The Employer's Voice

A Guide to Initiating Difficult Conversations
in Today's Workforce

LAURA SMITH

ISBN: 979-8-3462-4501-8

DEDICATION

*To every leader, manager, and team member who has ever felt the
weight of an uncomfortable conversation waiting to be had, this
book is for you. May it serve as a guide to empathy, courage, and
growth in the pursuit of better workplaces.*

*And to those who have taught me the value of listening,
understanding, and facing hard truths head-on — thank you for
inspiring this journey.*

CONTENTS

INTRODUCTION

In a fast-evolving work environment, effective communication has become one of the most valuable skills. Beyond the basics of relaying information or collaborating on projects, professionals today need to handle a wide range of conversations that can be sensitive, challenging, and sometimes uncomfortable. *The Employer's Voice: A Guide to Initiating Difficult Conversations in Today's Workforce* is designed to equip readers with the tools, strategies, and mindset required to tackle these conversations head-on, transforming them from dreaded interactions into powerful opportunities for growth, understanding, and improvement.

This book acknowledges that while technology and globalization have brought us closer, they've also introduced new complexities to workplace communication. Diverse teams with varied backgrounds, perspectives, and cultural values contribute to a richer environment but can also lead to misunderstandings and conflicts if communication isn't handled thoughtfully. Moreover, as remote and hybrid work have become the norm, we're faced with new challenges: deciphering tone over email, managing feedback in virtual settings, and maintaining team morale through digital interactions. In this context, the ability to address issues constructively and respectfully has never been more critical.

The Changing Nature of Workplace Conversations

The workplace of today differs substantially from even a decade ago. Issues like diversity, equity, and inclusion (DEI); mental health; personal boundaries; and work-life balance are at the forefront of organizational conversations. Employees are more likely than ever to speak openly about their values, and companies are expected to support them in creating an environment where they feel respected and heard. Yet, many of these topics are inherently personal, potentially sensitive, and can be challenging to address without guidance.

Alongside these changes, today's professionals have higher expectations for transparency, feedback, and growth within their roles. An annual review is no longer sufficient; employees want ongoing feedback and open channels to discuss their performance, goals, and development. These dialogues are essential to fostering engagement, but they also require a level of trust and skill that doesn't always come naturally.

This shift highlights the need for everyone—from entry-level employees to seasoned managers—to learn how to navigate difficult conversations with confidence and empathy. Whether you're delivering feedback, discussing career growth, addressing workplace conflicts, or having a candid conversation about personal boundaries, understanding *how* to communicate effectively in these moments is essential.

The Risks of Avoiding Difficult Conversations

Avoiding difficult conversations might feel like the safest path in the short term, but it often leads to long-term consequences. Misunderstandings can fester, productivity may suffer, and team morale can decline when issues are left unaddressed. For example, a manager who sidesteps discussions around poor performance may inadvertently enable poor habits, affecting team dynamics and overall productivity. Similarly, an employee who feels unheard or undervalued may disengage, impacting their work quality and their willingness to collaborate.

By sidestepping difficult conversations, we miss out on opportunities to address issues, learn from different perspectives, and foster a culture of open communication and trust. In contrast, addressing challenging topics proactively can enhance understanding, resolve conflicts, and build stronger professional relationships.

Why This Book?

The Employer's Voice is more than just a guide to navigating challenging workplace dialogues—it's a toolkit for developing a critical skill that can improve every aspect of professional life. Each chapter delves into specific types of conversations commonly encountered in the workplace, from delivering feedback and discussing career aspirations to addressing cultural sensitivities and handling conflict resolution.

What sets this book apart is its blend of practical strategies, real-life examples, and exercises designed to help readers internalize and apply these skills. Each conversation type is broken down into manageable steps that anyone can follow, regardless of their experience level. By grounding these techniques in empathy and active listening, the book ensures that readers not only become more confident communicators but also foster environments where respect, openness, and collaboration are the norms.

Key Components You'll Discover

1. **Preparation Techniques**: How to set clear goals, anticipate reactions, and mentally prepare for conversations that could become emotional or tense.

2. **Empathetic Listening**: Tools for truly hearing and understanding the other person's perspective, even when it differs from your own.

3. **Feedback Models**: Practical frameworks like the SBI (Situation-Behavior-Impact) model that help structure constructive feedback and make challenging conversations easier to handle.

4. **Cultural Sensitivity**: Insights on how to approach conversations with individuals from diverse backgrounds, recognizing and respecting different communication styles.

5. **Conflict Management**: Steps for de-escalating tense interactions and finding win-win solutions that strengthen professional relationships.

6. **Remote Communication Challenges**: Tips for effective virtual communication in remote and hybrid work environments, including maintaining rapport and managing digital misunderstandings.

Building a Culture of Open Communication

Beyond personal development, the skills covered in this book are foundational to creating a workplace culture where open communication is encouraged and celebrated. A culture that prioritizes transparent dialogue helps employees feel safe to speak up, brings teams closer, and drives higher engagement. It reduces misunderstandings, mitigates the buildup of tension, and leads to faster resolution of conflicts and misunderstandings.

Managers and leaders will find this book especially valuable, as they play a central role in setting the tone for communication within their teams. Leaders who model open, respectful dialogue encourage their employees to do the same, creating a ripple effect throughout the organization.

Who This Book Is For

The Employer's Voice is designed for anyone navigating today's workplace, from entry-level employees to senior executives. Whether you're looking to improve your feedback skills, address performance concerns, or build a more inclusive team environment, this guide provides the knowledge and skills to handle these moments with confidence and empathy.

In a world where professional success increasingly depends on effective communication, *How to Say It* is a roadmap to developing one of the most important skills for thriving in any workplace. Through clear strategies, relatable examples, and actionable exercises, this book invites readers to embrace the art of difficult conversations and transform these challenges into opportunities for growth.

1

UNDERSTANDING THE IMPORTANCE
OF DIFFICULT CONVERSATIONS

In every professional journey, there comes a point when difficult
conversations are unavoidable. These conversations can range from
addressing performance issues to discussing interpersonal conflicts or
talking about sensitive topics like personal boundaries, mental health, or
cultural differences. Despite their importance, many people avoid
difficult conversations due to fear, discomfort, or a lack of confidence.
However, evading these discussions often leads to greater challenges
down the line—unresolved issues can fester, misunderstandings deepen,
and relationships within the team can suffer. This chapter sets the
foundation by exploring why embracing difficult conversations is critical
to personal growth, team dynamics, and overall organizational health.

Why Difficult Conversations Matter

Difficult conversations may be uncomfortable, but they are crucial for
clarity, growth, and maintaining a healthy workplace environment.
Addressing problems directly helps to prevent small misunderstandings
from turning into larger conflicts and allows teams to operate more
transparently and productively. By engaging in open dialogue, we not
only resolve specific issues but also build a foundation of trust that
enhances teamwork and collaboration.

Some of the primary reasons difficult conversations are essential include:

1. **Creating a Culture of Transparency**: When difficult conversations are normalized, it signals that transparency is valued. A transparent workplace reduces confusion, promotes honesty, and encourages people to communicate more openly about their needs, concerns, and expectations.

2. **Preventing Miscommunication and Conflict**: Small misunderstandings can escalate if left unaddressed. Initiating these conversations early on allows for clarification, helping to prevent resentment and interpersonal conflicts.

3. **Supporting Personal and Professional Growth**: Difficult conversations often highlight areas for improvement or provide constructive feedback. This can be a powerful catalyst for personal development, allowing employees to understand their strengths and weaknesses and work towards becoming better professionals.

4. **Building Trust and Respect**: Addressing issues directly and respectfully fosters trust. Colleagues who feel heard and understood are more likely to respect one another, creating a more supportive and cohesive work environment.

Example: Consider a manager who notices that one of their team members has been missing deadlines. Avoiding the topic may lead to ongoing project delays and strain relationships with other team members. However, having a direct conversation could uncover underlying issues—perhaps the employee is struggling with time management or feels overloaded. By addressing the issue, the manager not only finds a solution but also demonstrates support for the employee's growth.

Common Reasons We Avoid Difficult Conversations

Despite the benefits, many people find themselves reluctant to initiate difficult conversations. Understanding why we avoid these situations can help us overcome the barriers to initiating open dialogue.

1. **Fear of Conflict or Emotional Reactions**: Many people are uncomfortable with confrontation, fearing that the conversation may become heated or emotional. This fear can lead to avoidance, especially if one expects a defensive or negative reaction.

2. **Concern About Damaging Relationships**: Professionals often worry that addressing sensitive issues might damage working relationships, leading to tension or discomfort in future interactions.

3. **Uncertainty About How to Approach the Topic**: Without clear guidance, people may feel lost on how to begin the conversation or express their thoughts effectively, leading to procrastination.

4. **Perfectionism and People-Pleasing Tendencies**: Individuals who want to be liked or who have perfectionist tendencies may avoid difficult conversations out of a desire to maintain a flawless or agreeable image. They may also feel that initiating criticism or feedback goes against their nature.

Exercise: Take a few minutes to reflect on a recent difficult conversation you avoided or postponed. Write down the primary reason you felt hesitant to engage in the conversation. Then, list one benefit that might have come from addressing it earlier. This reflection can help build awareness of personal patterns in handling tough topics.

Psychological Foundations of Effective Conversations

The psychology behind difficult conversations reveals how emotions, biases, and our perceptions of others affect our willingness to engage. Having an awareness of these psychological factors can help prepare us to face these conversations with a mindset focused on understanding and mutual respect.

1. **Trust as the Foundation of Communication**: Trust is essential in any professional relationship, as it creates a sense of safety and

openness. Without trust, people may assume defensive or guarded positions in conversation, limiting the potential for productive outcomes. Trust is built through consistent, honest interactions and a demonstrated willingness to listen.

2. **Emotional Intelligence**: Emotional intelligence—the ability to recognize and manage one's own emotions, as well as empathize with others—plays a key role in navigating difficult conversations. Those with high emotional intelligence are more likely to approach these situations calmly and respond constructively to emotional reactions.

3. **The Role of Perspective-Taking**: Being able to see a situation from another person's point of view helps reduce misinterpretation and conflict. By understanding where the other person is coming from, you can approach the conversation in a way that respects their viewpoint, which fosters openness and reduces defensiveness.

Tip: If you're feeling particularly nervous before a conversation, take a few minutes to consider the other person's perspective. Ask yourself questions like, "What might they be feeling about this situation?" and "What factors might have influenced their actions?" This simple exercise can build empathy and help you enter the conversation with a mindset that encourages understanding.

Risks of Avoiding Difficult Conversations

Avoiding difficult conversations might provide a temporary sense of relief, but the long-term consequences can be detrimental. By choosing to sidestep issues, we allow minor problems to grow, which can lead to:

1. **Increased Tension and Resentment**: Unresolved issues can cause resentment to build over time, leading to a toxic work environment where people feel unsupported or misunderstood.

2. **Decreased Productivity and Morale**: When people feel that problems are ignored, motivation and morale can suffer. Employees may feel that their concerns aren't valued, which affects their commitment and productivity.

3. **Loss of Trust and Respect**: Avoiding difficult conversations can erode trust within a team. If employees or colleagues feel that you're unwilling to address issues, they may lose respect for you as a leader or teammate.

Example: Imagine a scenario where a manager consistently fails to address performance issues with an underperforming team member. Other team members might begin to feel demotivated, wondering why they should work hard if poor performance is tolerated. Over time, the entire team's productivity and morale can decline as a result of the manager's avoidance.

The Benefits of Embracing Difficult Conversations

Taking the initiative to engage in challenging conversations can lead to substantial positive outcomes for individuals and teams alike. By facing these moments with courage and a constructive attitude, we can achieve:

1. **Stronger, More Respectful Relationships**: Addressing issues directly builds mutual respect. When people feel that they can discuss challenges openly, relationships become stronger and more resilient.

2. **Greater Personal and Professional Growth**: Difficult conversations often involve feedback, self-reflection, and learning, all of which contribute to personal growth. By actively participating in these discussions, professionals develop the skills and insights needed to improve.

3. **Improved Team Collaboration and Cohesion**: When team members address and resolve conflicts, they develop a greater sense of trust and collaboration. Open communication reduces misunderstandings and promotes a stronger sense of unity within the team.

4. **A More Positive, Productive Work Culture**: Embracing difficult conversations sets a precedent for transparency and accountability within an organization. Teams with a culture of open

communication are often more productive, innovative, and engaged.

Practical Takeaways and Chapter Summary

This chapter has laid the groundwork for understanding why difficult conversations are essential and what's at stake if they are avoided. To summarize:

- **Acknowledge the Importance of Communication**: Understand that addressing difficult topics is crucial for building trust, maintaining transparency, and supporting growth in any workplace.

- **Recognize and Overcome Avoidance Tendencies**: Be mindful of the common reasons we avoid difficult conversations and work to recognize when avoidance may be affecting your professional relationships.

- **Develop Emotional Intelligence and Empathy**: Cultivating these skills allows for a more constructive and compassionate approach to challenging topics.

- **Focus on Long-Term Benefits**: Remember that while difficult conversations may be uncomfortable in the short term, they contribute to a more supportive and productive workplace over time.

In the next chapters, we'll delve into practical strategies for initiating these conversations, including techniques for preparation, empathy, and feedback that will guide you through a variety of challenging topics you may encounter in today's employment world. By learning these tools, you'll be ready to approach each difficult conversation with confidence, clarity, and the skill to create positive change in your workplace.

2

PREPARING FOR A DIFFICULT CONVERSATION

Preparation is one of the most crucial steps in handling difficult conversations. The more thought and structure you put into preparing, the greater the chances of achieving a positive outcome. Whether you're addressing performance concerns, discussing team dynamics, or tackling personal boundaries, setting the right foundation is essential for navigating these interactions effectively.

In this chapter, we will cover how to prepare yourself mentally and emotionally, define the goals of the conversation, consider the other person's perspective, and choose the best timing and setting. We'll also look at practical exercises like role-playing and scripting, which can build your confidence and ensure that you're ready to handle even the toughest topics with clarity and empathy.

The Importance of Preparation in Difficult Conversations

Preparation can mean the difference between a constructive, empathetic discussion and a defensive, emotional confrontation. When you prepare effectively, you not only feel more in control, but you also create an environment that encourages openness and minimizes misunderstandings. Proper preparation helps you approach the conversation with clarity, empathy, and confidence, all of which are essential for a positive outcome.

Benefits of thorough preparation include:

1. **Clarified Goals and Objectives:** When you know what you want to achieve, you're more likely to guide the conversation in a productive direction.

2. **Reduced Emotional Reactivity:** Preparation allows you to process any strong emotions in advance, which helps you stay calm and focused during the discussion.

3. **Increased Empathy and Understanding:** Taking time to consider the other person's perspective helps you anticipate their reactions and approach the conversation with compassion.

4. **Greater Confidence and Poise:** Practicing what you plan to say and how you'll respond to potential challenges makes you feel more secure and reduces anxiety.

Example Scenario: Imagine a manager who is preparing to give critical feedback to an employee whose recent work has been below expectations. Without preparation, the manager might come across as frustrated or overly critical, leading to a defensive reaction from the employee. However, by preparing specific examples and thinking through the employee's potential responses, the manager can guide the conversation in a constructive direction.

Step 1: Setting Clear Goals and Defining Success

One of the first steps in preparing for a difficult conversation is to clarify your goals. What do you hope to accomplish by having this discussion? Are you looking to address a behavioral issue, improve a working relationship, or align on expectations for a project? Having a clear objective helps you stay focused and prevents the conversation from veering off course.

Consider different types of goals:

1. **Behavioral Change:** If you're addressing a specific behavior, make sure you can describe what the change would look like. For

example, if you want an employee to improve their punctuality, define the expectations around timeliness.

2. **Increased Understanding:** Sometimes, the goal is simply to improve mutual understanding. For instance, if a team member's cultural background influences their approach to teamwork, a conversation about their values may lead to a better understanding of their unique perspective.

3. **Improved Performance:** When discussing performance, set clear, actionable objectives that can be measured over time. Define what improved performance would look like in concrete terms.

Step 2: Anticipating the Other Person's Perspective and Reactions

A critical part of preparation is taking time to consider the other person's perspective. What might they be thinking or feeling about the topic? What objections or concerns might they have? Understanding their viewpoint helps you approach the conversation with empathy and anticipate potential reactions, allowing you to respond in a supportive and non-defensive manner.

Consider these key questions:

1. **What Motivates the Other Person?** Knowing their professional or personal goals can help frame the conversation in a way that resonates with them.

2. **What Challenges Might They Be Facing?** Reflecting on any stressors or barriers they might be experiencing allows you to approach the topic with empathy.

3. **How Might They React?** Anticipating their possible responses (defensiveness, anger, confusion) enables you to mentally prepare and respond calmly.

Example: If you're preparing to discuss a recurring issue with a colleague who's known to be sensitive to criticism, consider starting the conversation by acknowledging their strengths or contributions to the team. This approach can make them feel valued and more open to receiving feedback.

Step 3: Choosing the Right Timing and Setting

The timing and setting of a difficult conversation can significantly influence its outcome. A rushed, poorly timed conversation can exacerbate tensions, while a thoughtfully chosen moment and environment can create a sense of safety and openness.

Timing Considerations:

1. **Avoid High-Stress Periods:** If the person is under significant stress due to project deadlines, a personal crisis, or other challenges, consider postponing the conversation.

2. **Choose a Quiet, Private Environment:** Difficult conversations require privacy, so make sure the setting allows for confidential dialogue.

3. **Allocate Enough Time:** Don't schedule a difficult conversation right before another commitment. Give both parties enough time to express themselves fully.

Setting Examples:

1. **In-Person:** For sensitive or complex topics, in-person conversations are usually best. A face-to-face meeting allows for greater nuance in body language and tone.

2. **Video Conference:** If remote work prevents an in-person meeting, a video call is preferable to a phone call, as it allows for visual cues and feels more personal.

3. **Phone Call:** Only choose a phone call if an immediate response is necessary or if other methods are unavailable. Without visual cues, misunderstandings are more likely.

Step 4: Structuring the Conversation

Outlining a structure for the conversation can help you stay focused and ensure that you cover all necessary points. While the flow of the discussion may shift, having a basic framework in mind allows you to guide the conversation back on track if it veers off course.

A common structure might look like this:

1. **Opening:** Start with a positive, neutral, or empathetic statement to set a collaborative tone.

2. **Introduce the Issue:** Clearly and objectively state the reason for the conversation.

3. **Describe the Impact:** Explain how the issue is affecting you, the team, or the organization.

4. **Encourage Dialogue:** Invite the other person to share their thoughts, perspective, or concerns.

5. **Seek Solutions Together:** Collaborate on potential solutions, ideally arriving at a mutually agreed-upon course of action.

6. **Summarize and Close:** Recap the main points and outline any follow-up steps to ensure accountability and clarity.

Step 5: Practicing Through Role-Playing and Scripting

Role-playing and scripting can be valuable techniques for preparing emotionally and mentally for a difficult conversation. They allow you to practice delivering your points and prepare for a variety of reactions, so you're less likely to be caught off guard.

Role-Playing Tips:

1. **Find a Partner:** Ask a trusted friend or colleague to role-play the conversation with you, taking on the role of the other person. This practice can provide valuable feedback on your tone, wording, and body language.

2. **Simulate Reactions:** Ask your partner to simulate different reactions (defensiveness, anger, or confusion), so you can practice responding calmly and constructively.

3. **Reflect and Adjust:** After role-playing, take notes on areas where

you struggled or felt uncertain, then adjust your approach as needed.

Scripting Example: If you're addressing a performance issue, try scripting a few key points in advance, such as:

1. **Opening:** "I appreciate all the effort you've been putting into the team's projects. I wanted to have a conversation today about some of the challenges we've been facing."

2. **Describing the Issue:** "I've noticed that the last few projects have been submitted past the deadline, which has affected the team's ability to stay on schedule."

3. **Encouraging Dialogue:** "I'd love to hear your thoughts on what might be contributing to the delays. Are there any obstacles you're encountering?"

While it's essential to remain flexible, having a rough outline can help you stay focused and reduce nerves.

Step 6: Managing Your Own Emotions

One of the most challenging aspects of a difficult conversation is managing your own emotional responses. Going into a conversation with unresolved emotions, such as frustration or disappointment, can color your tone and make it harder to communicate effectively. Techniques like self-reflection, mindfulness, and re-framing your mindset can help.

1. **Self-Reflection:** Ask yourself why this conversation feels challenging. Are you worried about the other person's reaction? Are you afraid of the potential impact on your relationship? Identifying your own emotions can help you address them before entering the conversation.

2. **Mindfulness:** Practicing mindfulness can help you stay calm and focused. Deep breathing exercises, progressive muscle relaxation, or a quick mindfulness exercise before the conversation can help regulate any anxiety or stress.

3. **Reframe Your Mindset:** Instead of seeing the conversation as a confrontation, try to view it as a collaborative problem-solving exercise. This mindset shift can reduce your own defensiveness and encourage a more open, constructive discussion.

Step 7: Preparing for Potential Outcomes

While you can't control the other person's responses, you can prepare yourself for a variety of potential outcomes. Think about possible directions the conversation might take and how you would handle each one. If the person becomes defensive, how will you de-escalate? If they don't seem receptive to feedback, what's your backup plan? Having a few contingency strategies in place ensures that you're ready for whatever happens.

Example Contingencies:

1. **If They Become Defensive:** Gently restate your intention to understand their perspective and find a solution together.

2. **If They Agree with No Commitment to Change:** Reiterate the importance of the issue and, if necessary, outline follow-up steps or additional support measures.

3. **If They Shut Down:** Offer a pause or suggest scheduling a follow-up to allow them time to process the conversation.

Summary and Key Takeaways

Preparing for a difficult conversation is a multifaceted process that involves clarifying your objectives, understanding the other person's perspective, choosing the right time and setting, and practicing your approach. By investing time in these preparatory steps, you're setting the stage for a more constructive, empathetic, and productive dialogue.

Key Takeaways:

- **Define Clear Goals:** Know what you want to accomplish and how you'll measure success.

- **Consider the Other Person's Perspective:** Anticipate their reactions and prepare to respond with empathy.

- **Select the Right Time and Setting:** Find a private, unhurried space where both parties feel comfortable.

- **Use Role-Playing and Scripting:** Practicing your delivery can reduce anxiety and improve your confidence.

- **Manage Your Emotions:** Take steps to regulate your own emotions before entering the conversation.

- **Prepare for Different Outcomes:** Think through possible directions the conversation might take and how you'll respond to each.

In the next chapter, we'll dive into effective listening and empathy, exploring how these skills can create a supportive atmosphere that fosters open dialogue and understanding during difficult conversations. With solid preparation and a commitment to empathetic listening, you'll be well-equipped to handle even the toughest topics in the workplace.

3

EFFECTIVE LISTENING AND EMPATHY

One of the most powerful skills you can bring to a difficult conversation is the ability to listen effectively and demonstrate empathy. Listening isn't merely waiting for your turn to speak—it's an active, engaged process that requires focus, patience, and an open mind. When paired with empathy, effective listening can defuse tension, foster trust, and pave the way for a productive exchange of ideas.

In this chapter, we'll explore techniques and practices that will help you become a more attentive listener and demonstrate empathy, even when the conversation is challenging. We'll discuss reflective listening, empathy-building exercises, strategies for managing your reactions, and tips for responding thoughtfully. By developing these skills, you can create an environment where the other person feels understood and respected, which encourages open, honest communication and leads to better outcomes.

The Role of Active Listening in Difficult Conversations

Active listening is the foundation of any meaningful conversation. It involves focusing entirely on the speaker, absorbing their words, and responding in a way that shows you truly understand their perspective. In difficult conversations, active listening is especially valuable because it helps prevent misunderstandings, shows respect, and encourages a cooperative atmosphere.

The benefits of active listening in difficult conversations include:

1. **Reducing Defensiveness**: When people feel heard, they are less likely to respond defensively, making it easier to address challenging topics.

2. **Improving Mutual Understanding**: Active listening helps clarify each person's viewpoint, which reduces the risk of misinterpretation.

3. **Building Trust and Respect**: Consistently listening to others' perspectives shows that you value their input, which strengthens relationships.

4. **Encouraging Open Dialogue**: People are more likely to share honestly if they feel that their thoughts and emotions are genuinely valued.

Example Scenario: Consider a team leader who is discussing a project delay with a team member. By actively listening, the leader learns that the delay was caused by an unforeseen issue in the workflow, rather than negligence. This understanding changes the tone of the conversation from one of frustration to one of problem-solving, as they work together to find ways to prevent future delays.

Reflective Listening Techniques

Reflective listening is a technique that involves repeating back what the other person has said in your own words. This practice shows that you're not only hearing their words but also interpreting their meaning. Reflective listening helps clarify the other person's message, validates their feelings, and confirms your understanding.

Reflective Listening Steps:

1. **Listen Fully**: Focus entirely on the speaker without interrupting or thinking about your response.

2. **Summarize or Paraphrase**: After the person finishes speaking, summarize what they said in your own words. This confirms your

understanding and allows them to correct any misunderstandings.

3. **Acknowledge Emotions**: Reflect not only the content of what they said but also the emotions they might be feeling. For example, if they sound frustrated, you might say, "It sounds like this situation has been really stressful for you."

Example Response: When a colleague expresses frustration about feeling left out of project updates, a reflective listener might respond: "So you're feeling out of the loop with the project updates, and that's been frustrating for you. Is that right?" This statement validates the colleague's feelings and encourages them to open up further.

Developing Empathy: Putting Yourself in Their Shoes

Empathy goes beyond understanding someone's words; it's about feeling what they're feeling and seeing things from their perspective. Empathy helps you connect on a deeper level, making the conversation feel more personal and supportive. When people sense empathy, they are more likely to trust you, share openly, and consider your perspective as well.

To build empathy, practice the following:

1. **Imagine Their Perspective**: Before the conversation, take a moment to consider the other person's point of view. Ask yourself questions like, "What might they be going through?" or "What challenges could they be facing?"

2. **Acknowledge Their Feelings**: Use statements that show you recognize their emotions, such as "I can see that this is upsetting for you," or "It sounds like you've been under a lot of pressure."

3. **Express Understanding**: If you can relate to their experience, share a personal story or comment that shows you understand. However, avoid shifting the focus to your own experiences.

Example: A manager discussing feedback with an employee might say, "I understand that receiving critical feedback can be tough. I've been there too, and I know it's not easy to hear. I just want you to know that this conversation is about helping you succeed in the long term."

Responding vs. Reacting

A key aspect of both listening and empathy is the ability to respond thoughtfully rather than reacting impulsively. In difficult conversations, emotions can run high, and it's easy to react defensively or emotionally. However, reacting without thought can escalate tensions and close off communication.

To respond instead of react:

1. **Pause Before Responding**: Take a deep breath or count to three before speaking. This brief pause can prevent you from reacting emotionally and allow you to respond with intention.

2. **Acknowledge and Validate**: When someone expresses an emotion, acknowledge it without judgment. For example, "I can see why you'd feel that way," or "Thank you for sharing how you feel about this."

3. **Use Neutral Language**: Avoid language that could come across as accusatory or judgmental. Instead of saying, "You always miss deadlines," say, "I noticed that a few deadlines have been missed recently."

Example: If an employee reacts defensively to feedback, a manager who practices thoughtful responding might say, "I appreciate your perspective, and I understand this may feel surprising. I'd like us to look at how we can work together to find solutions."

Dealing with Emotional Responses: Staying Calm and Supportive

Difficult conversations often bring out strong emotions, and it's not uncommon for someone to react with anger, sadness, or frustration. Managing these emotions requires a calm, supportive presence and a focus on de-escalation. Here are some techniques to keep the conversation constructive even when emotions run high:

1. **Acknowledge the Emotion**: Recognize and validate the other person's feelings without attempting to "fix" them immediately.

Often, people just want to be heard.

2. **Stay Neutral and Composed**: Use a steady tone of voice and avoid mirroring negative emotions. If the other person raises their voice or appears angry, maintaining a calm demeanor can help de-escalate the situation.

3. **Offer a Pause if Needed**: If emotions are overwhelming, suggest a brief break to allow both of you to regroup. Sometimes, stepping away for a few minutes can restore calm and refocus the conversation.

Example: If a team member begins to cry during a conversation about a difficult project, you might say, "I can see that this topic is really emotional for you. Would you like to take a few minutes, or would you prefer to continue? I'm here to listen."

Asking Open-Ended Questions

One of the best ways to encourage openness is by asking open-ended questions. These questions invite the other person to share their thoughts and feelings freely, rather than giving simple "yes" or "no" answers. Open-ended questions foster a deeper understanding and help you gather valuable context that might not surface otherwise.

Examples of Open-Ended Questions:

1. **"Can you tell me more about how you're feeling about this situation?"**

2. **"What do you think could help improve this situation?"**

3. **"How has this issue impacted your work or your experience on the team?"**

4. **"What would a successful outcome look like to you?"**

By asking these kinds of questions, you show a genuine interest in the other person's perspective and create space for them to express their concerns fully.

Validating and Affirming: Making the Other Person Feel Heard

Validation is a powerful tool in difficult conversations. When people feel that their feelings are acknowledged and understood, they are more likely to engage openly and constructively. Validating does not necessarily mean agreeing; it simply means recognizing and respecting the other person's experience.

To validate someone's perspective:

1. **Acknowledge Their Experience**: Use phrases like, "I can see why you'd feel that way," or "It sounds like this has been really challenging for you."

2. **Express Appreciation**: Thank them for sharing their thoughts or feelings, especially if the topic is difficult or sensitive.

3. **Avoid Dismissing or Minimizing**: Don't downplay their feelings or offer solutions right away. Instead, let them know that their experience matters to you.

Example: If a colleague expresses frustration about a lack of support, you might say, "I understand that feeling unsupported can be really frustrating. I appreciate you bringing this to my attention."

Summary and Key Takeaways

Effective listening and empathy are essential components of a productive difficult conversation. By focusing on active listening, demonstrating empathy, and responding thoughtfully, you create a supportive environment that fosters trust and openness.

Key Takeaways:

- **Practice Reflective Listening**: Summarize and paraphrase what the other person says to confirm your understanding and demonstrate that you're listening actively.

- **Build Empathy**: Put yourself in the other person's shoes to understand their perspective and validate their feelings.

- **Respond, Don't React**: Pause before responding to prevent emotional reactions, and choose language that promotes calm and clarity.

- **Ask Open-Ended Questions**: Encourage the other person to share their thoughts fully and invite them to collaborate on solutions.

- **Validate Their Experience**: Acknowledge their feelings and show appreciation for their willingness to engage in the conversation.

In the next chapter, we'll dive into strategies for providing constructive feedback, focusing on techniques for delivering feedback that is clear, actionable, and supportive. By combining effective listening and empathy with thoughtful feedback, you'll be well-equipped to handle difficult conversations with skill and confidence.

4

THE LANGUAGE OF
CONSTRUCTIVE FEEDBACK

Feedback is a fundamental part of professional development, yet delivering it can be challenging. Constructive feedback—feedback that is both specific and actionable—has the power to inspire improvement, build trust, and reinforce positive behaviors. Unfortunately, without the right approach, feedback can feel like criticism or create defensiveness, potentially harming relationships and discouraging open dialogue.

In this chapter, we'll explore how to deliver feedback that is constructive, focused on growth, and aligned with the needs and goals of the recipient. We'll dive into proven techniques, including the SBI (Situation-Behavior-Impact) model, the "sandwich" method, and tips for managing your tone and timing. By mastering these techniques, you'll be able to provide feedback that is clear, respectful, and empowering.

The Importance of Constructive Feedback

Constructive feedback is essential for any productive workplace. It provides employees and colleagues with the insights they need to improve their performance, align with organizational expectations, and grow professionally. When feedback is delivered with care and clarity, it becomes a tool for building trust, strengthening relationships, and fostering a culture of continuous improvement.

Key Benefits of Constructive Feedback:

1. **Promotes Personal and Professional Growth:** Feedback helps individuals recognize areas where they excel and identify opportunities for improvement.

2. **Enhances Team Performance:** When everyone understands their strengths and areas for growth, teams function more cohesively and productively.

3. **Builds Trust and Open Communication:** Thoughtful feedback encourages honesty, openness, and a willingness to discuss difficult topics.

4. **Reinforces Positive Behaviors:** Constructive feedback isn't just about addressing mistakes; it's also a powerful tool for acknowledging and encouraging positive actions.

Example: Imagine a team member who is a diligent worker but often struggles with meeting deadlines. By providing constructive feedback focused on specific instances and offering solutions, you can help them develop stronger time-management skills, benefitting both the individual and the team.

Preparing for a Feedback Conversation

Before giving feedback, it's important to prepare. Unplanned or rushed feedback can feel harsh and may lack the clarity needed for actionable improvement. Here are some steps to consider as you prepare:

1. **Define the Purpose of Your Feedback:** Clarify what you want to achieve. Are you addressing a specific behavior, reinforcing a positive action, or helping someone meet performance expectations?

2. **Identify the Specific Behavior:** Feedback should be as specific as possible. Instead of generalities, think about precise instances or behaviors you want to address.

3. **Consider Timing and Setting:** Timing matters when delivering feedback. Try to offer feedback close to the behavior or outcome, but not in the heat of the moment if emotions are high. Choose a private, distraction-free setting where both parties can focus on the conversation.

Example: If a colleague regularly arrives late to meetings, providing feedback directly after the meeting might make them feel embarrassed in front of others. Waiting until a private, one-on-one moment allows you to address the issue respectfully and constructively.

The SBI (Situation-Behavior-Impact) Model

The Situation-Behavior-Impact (SBI) model is a structured feedback method that helps you communicate clearly and objectively. By focusing on specific situations and behaviors, it reduces the likelihood of triggering defensiveness and ensures that feedback remains constructive.

Using the SBI Model:

1. **Situation:** Start by describing the specific context where the behavior occurred. Providing context helps the person understand exactly what you're referring to.

2. **Behavior:** Describe the specific behavior you observed without judgment or exaggeration.

3. **Impact:** Explain the effect this behavior had on you, the team, or the project. This step connects the behavior to a larger context, making the feedback more relevant and meaningful.

Example: "SBI Feedback for a Colleague Who Misses Deadlines"

1. **Situation:** "In the last project update meeting…"

2. **Behavior:** "I noticed that your report wasn't ready by the deadline we had agreed on."

3. **Impact:** "This delayed the team's ability to move forward with their parts, which put extra pressure on everyone to catch up."

The SBI model is powerful because it focuses on the impact of the behavior, not on personal attributes, keeping the conversation objective and productive.

The "Sandwich" Method for Delivering Feedback

The "sandwich" method is another popular approach that involves layering constructive feedback between positive comments. While this method should be used thoughtfully (to avoid the feedback sounding forced or disingenuous), it can be effective for balancing criticism with encouragement.

How to Use the Sandwich Method:

1. **Start with Positive Feedback:** Begin by acknowledging something positive about the person's performance or behavior to set a supportive tone.

2. **Provide Constructive Feedback:** Deliver the specific feedback, being clear and direct about the behavior and the desired change.

3. **End on a Positive Note:** Conclude with encouragement or a positive statement about their potential to improve, reinforcing your confidence in their abilities.

Example: "Your attention to detail in the last report was impressive. However, I noticed that it was submitted a bit past the deadline, which caused a delay for the team. I'm confident that with a bit of time management adjustment, you'll be able to maintain that quality while meeting deadlines more consistently."

While the sandwich method can help soften critical feedback, be careful not to dilute the message. If there's a pressing issue, focus on making the feedback clear and actionable rather than overly cushioned.

Delivering Positive Feedback: Reinforcing Strengths and Successes

Feedback isn't always about improvement—reinforcing positive behaviors is just as important for motivation and morale. Recognizing and encouraging strengths encourages people to continue those behaviors and helps build a positive workplace culture.

Tips for Delivering Positive Feedback:

1. **Be Specific:** Instead of vague praise, focus on specific actions or behaviors.

2. **Connect to Impact:** Show the person how their actions contributed to a successful outcome or positively affected the team.

3. **Encourage Continued Growth:** Use positive feedback as an opportunity to encourage further development.

Example: "I really appreciate how proactive you were in identifying the issue with our client's account. Your attention to detail prevented a larger problem and saved the team a lot of time. Please keep up this initiative—it really makes a difference."

Choosing Your Language: Avoiding Common Feedback Pitfalls

The language you use when delivering feedback can significantly impact how it is received. Avoiding certain phrases and word choices can help prevent defensiveness and encourage a more open, constructive response.

Common Pitfalls to Avoid:

1. **Avoid Absolutes:** Words like "always" and "never" can make feedback feel exaggerated or personal. Instead, focus on specific instances.

2. **Don't Overgeneralize:** Phrases like "You're disorganized" are vague and can be discouraging. Specific examples are more effective.

3. **Steer Clear of Judgmental Language:** Avoid words that could come across as accusatory or judgmental. Instead, focus on observations.

Managing Tone and Body Language

Nonverbal cues play a major role in how feedback is received. Body language, tone of voice, and eye contact all contribute to the perception of your message. A calm, neutral tone paired with open body language can make feedback feel more supportive and less intimidating.

Tips for Managing Tone and Body Language:

1. **Maintain Eye Contact:** This conveys that you're engaged and sincere.

2. **Keep an Open Posture:** Avoid crossing your arms, which can come across as defensive.

3. **Use a Calm, Steady Tone:** Avoid raising your voice or sounding overly critical. A steady tone helps keep the conversation calm and professional.

Encouraging Dialogue and Solution-Finding

Feedback should be a two-way conversation, not a lecture. Encourage the other person to share their perspective, ask questions, and participate in finding a solution. This approach fosters collaboration and demonstrates respect for their input.

How to Encourage Dialogue:

1. **Ask Open-Ended Questions:** Questions like "What challenges did you face with this project?" or "How do you think we can avoid this in the future?" invite them to share their viewpoint.

2. **Listen Actively:** Show that you value their perspective by listening without interrupting or judging.

3. **Collaborate on Solutions:** Work together to find strategies for improvement, making them feel empowered and engaged in the process.

Example: After giving feedback about missed deadlines, you might ask, "What do you think would help you stay on track with future projects?" This approach encourages them to take ownership of the solution.

Following Up After Feedback

Feedback doesn't end with the initial conversation. Following up ensures accountability, reinforces positive change, and shows that you're invested in their success. Schedule a check-in to review progress and offer support if needed.

Steps for Following Up:

1. **Set a Check-In Date:** Schedule a follow-up to discuss progress, whether it's in a week, a month, or the next review cycle.

2. **Acknowledge Improvement:** If you notice positive changes, recognize them to reinforce the behavior.

3. **Provide Ongoing Support:** Offer assistance or resources if they need further help.

Example: After discussing time management, follow up a few weeks later by saying, "I've noticed you've been meeting deadlines more consistently. Great work! How are you feeling about the new process?"

Summary and Key Takeaways

Constructive feedback is a powerful tool for professional growth, team cohesion, and productivity when done effectively. By focusing on specific behaviors, managing your tone, and encouraging dialogue, you can deliver feedback in a way that feels supportive and empowering.

Key Takeaways:

- **Use the SBI Model:** Structure feedback around specific situations, behaviors, and their impacts to keep it clear and objective.

- **Try the Sandwich Method Thoughtfully:** Balance critical feedback with positive reinforcement to create a supportive tone.

- **Be Mindful of Language and Tone:** Avoid judgmental or absolute language and manage your body language to prevent defensiveness.

- **Encourage Dialogue:** Make feedback a two-way conversation, inviting input and solution-finding.

- **Follow Up:** Reinforce positive changes by scheduling a follow-up to review progress and show ongoing support.

In the next chapter, we'll focus on how to approach conversations that require cultural sensitivity, helping you navigate diverse perspectives and foster an inclusive, respectful workplace. By combining constructive feedback with cultural awareness, you'll be well-prepared for today's globalized work environment.

5

ADDRESSING CULTURAL SENSITIVITY
IN COMMUNICATION

In today's globalized world, workplaces are more diverse than ever, encompassing individuals from a range of cultural backgrounds, belief systems, and communication styles. While this diversity enriches the work environment, it also brings challenges that require a heightened awareness of cultural differences. Being culturally sensitive in communication is crucial to fostering inclusivity, reducing misunderstandings, and building trust among team members. Addressing cultural sensitivity in workplace conversations goes beyond simple politeness—it's about understanding and respecting differences in values, norms, and communication styles.

In this chapter, we will explore the importance of cultural sensitivity in the workplace, offer strategies to help you communicate effectively across cultures, and provide practical tips for handling conversations where cultural perspectives may differ. By approaching these conversations with an open mind and a willingness to learn, you can create a more respectful, inclusive, and collaborative workplace.

Understanding Cultural Sensitivity

Cultural sensitivity is the awareness that each person's background and culture influence how they perceive, interpret, and respond to the world around them. In the workplace, this means recognizing that individuals from different backgrounds may have distinct approaches to communication, conflict resolution, feedback, and teamwork.

Key Aspects of Cultural Sensitivity:

1. **Awareness of Differences**: Understanding that everyone brings unique experiences and perspectives influenced by their cultural backgrounds.

2. **Respect for Diversity**: Valuing these differences as strengths and showing respect for each person's culture, beliefs, and communication style.

3. **Willingness to Adapt**: Being flexible in your approach to communication to accommodate and respect others' preferences.

Example: In some cultures, direct eye contact is considered a sign of respect, while in others, it may be perceived as challenging or aggressive. Understanding these differences can help you adjust your approach to build trust and avoid misinterpretations.

Why Cultural Sensitivity Matters in Communication

Cultural sensitivity is essential to creating a respectful and productive workplace. By embracing cultural differences, you contribute to a more inclusive environment where everyone feels valued and understood. When cultural sensitivity is prioritized, employees are more likely to engage openly, collaborate effectively, and contribute their best work.

Benefits of Cultural Sensitivity in the Workplace:

1. **Enhances Collaboration**: Respecting cultural differences builds stronger, more cooperative teams.

2. **Reduces Conflict**: When people understand each other's perspectives, there is less potential for misunderstandings and tension.

3. **Increases Innovation**: Diverse perspectives foster creativity and innovation, as people are exposed to new ideas and approaches.

4. **Promotes Employee Retention**: An inclusive culture where individuals feel respected increases job satisfaction and reduces turnover.

Example: A multicultural team might approach problem-solving from different angles due to varied cultural influences. When these perspectives are valued, the team is likely to come up with more innovative solutions.

Common Areas of Cultural Differences in Communication

Cultural differences can manifest in various ways, impacting communication styles, body language, attitudes toward hierarchy, and more. Recognizing these differences helps you navigate cross-cultural interactions with greater sensitivity and adaptability.

1. **Direct vs. Indirect Communication**: In some cultures (e.g., many Western cultures), direct communication is valued, with individuals encouraged to speak openly and directly. In other cultures, especially in parts of Asia and Latin America, indirect communication may be preferred, with people avoiding confrontation or expressing disagreement subtly.

2. **High-Context vs. Low-Context Communication**: High-context cultures (e.g., Japan, India) rely on implicit communication, where context, body language, and shared understanding are essential. Low-context cultures (e.g., the United States, Germany) emphasize explicit, clear communication where the message is primarily contained in the words spoken.

3. **Formality and Respect for Hierarchy**: In some cultures, formal language and respect for hierarchy are essential. For example, in many Asian cultures, it's customary to show deference to seniority or authority. In contrast, Western cultures often have a more egalitarian approach, where employees are encouraged to communicate openly with managers or executives.

4. **Body Language and Nonverbal Cues**: Gestures, eye contact, and

physical space preferences vary widely across cultures. For instance, while maintaining eye contact is seen as a sign of confidence in Western cultures, it can be considered disrespectful in certain Middle Eastern or East Asian cultures.

5. **Attitudes Toward Feedback**: Cultures differ in their approach to giving and receiving feedback. Some cultures (e.g., the Netherlands, Germany) value direct feedback, even if it's critical. Other cultures may prefer to offer feedback indirectly or focus primarily on positive aspects to avoid offense.

Example: A manager from a low-context, direct communication culture might unintentionally offend an employee from a high-context, indirect communication culture by being too straightforward in delivering feedback.

Strategies for Culturally Sensitive Communication

Navigating cultural differences requires intentionality, empathy, and adaptability. Here are some strategies to help you communicate more effectively with colleagues from diverse cultural backgrounds.

1. **Educate Yourself About Cultural Differences**: Familiarize yourself with common cultural communication styles and preferences. While it's impossible to know every detail, a basic understanding can go a long way in preventing misunderstandings.

2. **Ask Open-Ended Questions**: When in doubt, ask questions to clarify communication preferences. For example, "How do you prefer to receive feedback?" or "Is there a way you'd like us to handle meetings to make it comfortable for everyone?"

3. **Be Aware of Assumptions and Stereotypes**: Avoid making assumptions based on cultural stereotypes. Instead, treat each person as an individual and get to know their unique preferences.

4. **Practice Active Listening and Empathy**: Listen carefully to understand the other person's perspective without judgment.

Show empathy by acknowledging their experiences and adapting your communication style to meet them halfway.

5. **Be Mindful of Body Language and Tone**: Pay attention to your nonverbal cues and ensure they align with your words. Avoid gestures or expressions that may be perceived differently across cultures.

6. **Adapt Your Feedback Style**: Adjust your feedback style to accommodate different preferences. For example, you might use the "sandwich" method (positive feedback, constructive feedback, positive feedback) for individuals from cultures that value indirect communication.

Example: If you're working with a team member from a high-context culture, be mindful to offer context when giving instructions, rather than assuming they understand immediately. This approach helps prevent misunderstandings and promotes mutual understanding.

Approaching Cross-Cultural Conflicts

Conflicts can arise when cultural differences are misunderstood or ignored. Approaching these conflicts with cultural sensitivity can help resolve issues while maintaining respect for all parties involved.

Steps to Address Cross-Cultural Conflicts:

1. **Acknowledge the Conflict Without Blame**: Recognize that cultural misunderstandings are often unintentional and avoid assigning blame.

2. **Seek to Understand**: Ask open-ended questions to understand the other person's perspective. "Can you help me understand how you view this situation?"

3. **Clarify Intentions**: Explain your intentions to ensure the other person knows you mean no offense. Clarify any cultural differences that may have contributed to the misunderstanding.

4. **Focus on Solutions**: Work together to find a resolution that

respects both parties' cultural preferences. This may involve adjusting how tasks are assigned, feedback is given, or meetings are conducted.

Example: If two team members disagree due to differences in communication styles (direct vs. indirect), acknowledge the cultural basis for each style and explore how they can find a middle ground that respects both preferences.

Handling Sensitive Topics Across Cultures

Certain topics, such as feedback, personal boundaries, and career aspirations, can be more sensitive depending on cultural context. Being aware of cultural sensitivities helps you approach these conversations with respect and empathy.

1. **Feedback Conversations**: Tailor your feedback approach to the recipient's cultural preferences. In high-context cultures, a more indirect approach may be appreciated, such as framing feedback within positive statements. In cultures that value directness, provide feedback straightforwardly while maintaining respect.

   Example: When giving feedback to a team member from a culture that values face-saving, you might focus more on the positives and offer constructive suggestions subtly.

2. **Discussions About Personal Boundaries**: In cultures where personal boundaries are highly respected, discussing work-life balance or setting limits on after-hours communication is often necessary. In other cultures, colleagues might feel more comfortable blending work with personal interactions.

   Example: If you're working with someone from a culture that values personal space, be mindful of physical proximity and respect their personal boundaries in shared workspaces.

3. **Career Growth Conversations**: Different cultures may have distinct approaches to discussing career advancement. In some

cultures, discussing promotions or salary increases is considered forward or even impolite. In others, self-promotion and ambition are seen as positive qualities.

Example: When discussing career growth with a team member from a culture that values humility, focus on their accomplishments and contributions rather than encouraging self-promotion.

Building a Culturally Inclusive Team Environment

Creating a culture of inclusivity goes beyond individual interactions. By implementing team-wide practices that honor diversity and cultural sensitivity, you can create an environment where everyone feels valued and respected.

Strategies for Building an Inclusive Team:

1. **Set Ground Rules for Respectful Communication**: Establish team norms that encourage respect, active listening, and open dialogue. These guidelines serve as a reference point for managing cultural differences constructively.

2. **Encourage Knowledge Sharing**: Create opportunities for team members to share insights about their culture, if they're comfortable. This can be as simple as allowing individuals to introduce cultural customs or holiday traditions in team meetings.

3. **Celebrate Diversity in Team Events**: Incorporate cultural elements into team-building activities, such as celebrating international holidays or organizing cultural potlucks. These activities foster appreciation for diversity and create a more inclusive atmosphere.

4. **Provide Training on Cultural Sensitivity**: Formal training can be highly effective in helping team members understand and appreciate cultural differences. Offer resources, workshops, or guest speakers to build cultural awareness across the team.

5. **Model Cultural Sensitivity as a Leader**: Leaders set the tone for

inclusivity. By modeling cultural sensitivity in your communication and actions, you encourage others to do the same.

Example: A manager might schedule regular "cultural appreciation" sessions where team members can share about their background, traditions, or experiences, creating an environment of mutual respect and understanding.

Navigating Cultural Sensitivity in Remote or Global Teams

Remote teams and international collaborations add an extra layer of complexity to cultural sensitivity, as communication is often limited to digital channels. Without face-to-face interaction, it can be more challenging to pick up on subtle cues or clarify misunderstandings.

Tips for Cultural Sensitivity in Remote or Global Teams:

1. **Be Mindful of Time Zones**: Respect different time zones when scheduling meetings and avoid setting times that would be inconvenient for team members in other regions.

2. **Clarify Expectations**: Digital communication can sometimes lead to ambiguity. Be as clear and explicit as possible in emails or chat messages, as high-context cues may be lost.

3. **Use Inclusive Language**: Be mindful of regional phrases or idioms that may not translate across cultures. Aim for clear, straightforward language to avoid confusion.

4. **Encourage Video Calls for Important Conversations**: Video calls allow for nonverbal cues and a more personal connection, which can improve understanding in culturally diverse teams.

5. **Regularly Check In on Cultural Comfort**: Periodically ask remote team members if they feel comfortable with the team's communication style or if they have any suggestions for improvement.

Example: When holding a virtual meeting with a global team, a manager might use clear agendas and avoid slang, ensuring everyone can follow along regardless of cultural or linguistic differences.

Summary and Key Takeaways

Cultural sensitivity is essential for fostering an inclusive and respectful workplace. By understanding cultural differences in communication styles, adapting your approach, and promoting inclusivity, you can build stronger, more cooperative teams.

Key Takeaways:

- **Educate Yourself on Cultural Differences**: Be aware of common cultural communication norms, including preferences for direct or indirect communication.

- **Avoid Stereotyping**: Approach each person as an individual and avoid making assumptions based on culture alone.

- **Encourage Open Dialogue**: Create a safe space for team members to express their preferences and cultural insights.

- **Practice Empathy and Adaptability**: Demonstrate empathy by adapting your communication style to meet others' needs.

- **Model Inclusivity**: Lead by example, showing respect for cultural differences and encouraging inclusivity at every level.

In the next chapter, we'll discuss how to approach conversations specifically about performance, focusing on providing feedback, setting goals, and ensuring alignment with organizational expectations. By combining cultural sensitivity with effective performance conversations, you can foster a positive, growth-oriented workplace.

6

NAVIGATING CONVERSATIONS
ABOUT PERFORMANCE

Performance conversations are among the most challenging yet essential discussions in any workplace. When handled well, these conversations provide employees with clarity on expectations, constructive feedback, and pathways for development. They also enable managers and team members to address concerns before they become larger issues, thus promoting productivity and a positive work culture.

This chapter focuses on how to conduct productive performance conversations that foster improvement, engagement, and accountability. We'll explore techniques for setting a constructive tone, strategies for balancing positive and corrective feedback, and how to set measurable goals. Additionally, we'll cover approaches for managing sensitive topics, encouraging employee self-reflection, and following up to track progress. By the end of this chapter, you'll be equipped with tools and strategies to guide productive performance discussions, even in challenging situations.

The Purpose and Benefits of Performance Conversations

Performance conversations are a cornerstone of professional development and play an integral role in maintaining team alignment with organizational goals. While many associate these discussions with performance evaluations, they're also opportunities for encouragement, support, and engagement.

Benefits of Regular Performance Conversations:

1. **Clarify Expectations and Goals:** Regular discussions ensure that employees understand their role and what is expected of them.

2. **Provide Constructive Feedback:** Ongoing feedback allows employees to continuously improve, rather than waiting for an annual review to address issues.

3. **Encourage Personal Development:** Performance conversations highlight strengths and growth areas, guiding employees toward skill-building opportunities.

4. **Build Trust and Engagement:** Transparent discussions foster an open, trusting relationship between employees and managers, increasing engagement and motivation.

Example: A project manager who regularly discusses team members' performance not only helps them align with project goals but also provides timely support to help them improve or overcome challenges.

Preparing for a Performance Conversation

Preparation is essential for a productive performance conversation. Taking time to organize your thoughts, review relevant information, and set clear objectives helps you approach the discussion with confidence and structure.

Steps for Preparing a Performance Conversation:

1. **Review Performance Data:** Gather relevant information, such as project outcomes, metrics, and feedback from colleagues. Use specific data points rather than general observations to support your points.

2. **Define Clear Objectives:** Decide on the primary purpose of the conversation. Are you focusing on improvements, celebrating

achievements, or both? Clarify what you want to accomplish by the end of the discussion.

3. **Prepare Specific Examples:** Identify specific examples that illustrate the employee's strengths and areas for growth. Concrete examples help clarify your points and prevent misunderstandings.

4. **Plan for a Collaborative Discussion:** Prepare to invite the employee's input and perspective. This makes the conversation feel more balanced and allows them to actively engage in their development.

Example: Before discussing an employee's recent drop in productivity, review their recent tasks, deadlines, and any challenges they may have encountered. This shows the employee that you're informed and focused on specifics rather than assumptions.

Setting a Constructive Tone

The tone you set at the beginning of the conversation shapes how the employee will respond. By opening the conversation in a supportive, non-judgmental way, you create an environment where they feel comfortable discussing their challenges and open to feedback.

Tips for Setting a Constructive Tone:

1. **Start with Positive Acknowledgments:** Begin by recognizing the employee's achievements or contributions. This sets a balanced tone and demonstrates that you value their efforts.

2. **Use Open-Ended Language:** Encourage dialogue by using phrases like, "I'd like to discuss how we can support your growth" instead of "I need to talk to you about some issues."

3. **Express Confidence in Their Potential:** Reassure the employee that your feedback is intended to support their development. Statements like, "I believe you have a lot of potential in this area" can reinforce their motivation.

4. **Show Empathy:** Acknowledge any known challenges or pressures

they might be experiencing, such as high workload or a recent shift in responsibilities.

Example Opening Statement: "Thank you for your hard work on recent projects. I've noticed some areas where I think we can work together to help you reach your full potential. I'd love to hear your thoughts on your recent performance and discuss some ideas for moving forward."

Balancing Positive and Corrective Feedback

Providing a balance of positive and constructive feedback ensures that the conversation feels fair and supportive. Positive feedback reinforces strengths, while constructive feedback offers specific guidance for improvement.

Strategies for Balancing Feedback:

1. **Acknowledge Strengths First:** Begin by highlighting the employee's strengths or recent successes. This demonstrates that you recognize and value their contributions.

2. **Use the SBI Model for Constructive Feedback:** The Situation-Behavior-Impact model (introduced in Chapter 4) helps keep feedback specific and objective.

3. **End on a Positive Note:** Conclude the conversation by encouraging them to continue their strengths or by expressing confidence in their ability to improve.

Example: "You did a fantastic job managing the client presentation last week—your preparation really showed. I noticed, however, that there were a few last-minute adjustments that affected the team's workflow. Let's work on planning ahead to ensure everything runs smoothly in the future."

Setting Measurable Performance Goals with the SMART Framework

Performance goals provide a clear pathway for improvement and development. By setting SMART goals—Specific, Measurable,

Achievable, Relevant, and Time-bound—you create a structured roadmap for the employee to follow, making it easier to track their progress.

Components of SMART Goals:

1. **Specific:** Define the goal in clear, concrete terms.

2. **Measurable:** Identify how you'll measure success, whether through metrics or observable behaviors.

3. **Achievable:** Ensure the goal is realistic, considering their current role and resources.

4. **Relevant:** Align the goal with their role, team objectives, and broader organizational goals.

5. **Time-bound:** Set a timeline for achieving the goal, allowing for consistent check-ins and adjustments as needed.

Example SMART Goal:

"Improve project documentation by updating all reports weekly, with a summary provided to the team by Friday at 4 PM. This will help the team stay aligned on project progress and reduce misunderstandings."

Setting goals collaboratively can be especially motivating. Encourage the employee to suggest their own goals or adjustments to the proposed goals so that they feel personally invested in their development.

Encouraging Self-Reflection

Inviting employees to reflect on their performance before and during the conversation promotes accountability and self-awareness. By asking reflective questions, you encourage them to take ownership of their progress and to actively engage in finding solutions.

Reflective Questions to Encourage Self-Assessment:

1. **"What aspects of your role do you feel most confident about?"**

2. **"Are there any challenges you've encountered that you'd like support with?"**

3. **"What do you think went well in your recent projects, and where do you see room for improvement?"**

4. **"Are there any specific skills or resources you'd like to develop further?"**

By encouraging self-reflection, you empower employees to take an active role in their own development, helping them identify solutions that feel authentic and manageable.

Navigating Sensitive Topics with Empathy

Certain topics, such as frequent mistakes, lack of motivation, or interpersonal conflicts, can be difficult to address. When these topics arise, empathy and patience are essential. Approaching these conversations carefully can prevent the employee from feeling embarrassed or defensive.

Strategies for Handling Sensitive Topics:

1. **Acknowledge the Sensitivity:** Recognize that the topic may be challenging and approach it with understanding.

2. **Use Neutral Language:** Avoid judgmental language. Instead of saying, "You're often disorganized," say, "I've noticed that task prioritization has been challenging recently."

3. **Frame Feedback as Support:** Emphasize that your feedback is intended to help them overcome challenges. For example, "I'm here to support you as we work through this."

Example: If you need to discuss an employee's repeated mistakes, you might say, "I understand that handling multiple tasks can be overwhelming. Let's work together to find a way to streamline your workflow and reduce errors."

Encouraging Collaboration in Performance Improvement

For performance conversations to be effective, they should be collaborative. Instead of dictating solutions, invite the employee to contribute their own ideas on how they can improve. This approach fosters engagement and shows respect for their insight and knowledge of their role.

How to Foster Collaboration:

1. **Ask for Their Perspective:** Start by asking for their view on their performance, which can reveal their insights and self-awareness.

2. **Brainstorm Solutions Together:** Explore potential solutions as a team, allowing the employee to suggest ideas.

3. **Offer Support:** Discuss resources, training, or adjustments that could support their improvement efforts.

Example: After discussing time management challenges, you could ask, "What do you think would help you stay organized? Are there any tools or strategies that you find effective?"

Tracking Progress and Providing Ongoing Support

Performance improvement is a continuous process. Following up on agreed-upon goals shows that you're invested in the employee's growth and holds them accountable to their commitments. Regular check-ins also allow you to address any challenges early and provide additional support if necessary.

Steps for Effective Follow-Up:

1. **Schedule Regular Check-Ins:** Set periodic meetings to discuss progress, offer support, and adjust goals as needed.

2. **Recognize Improvements:** Acknowledge even small improvements to reinforce positive behavior and motivate further progress.

3. **Provide Additional Resources:** If the employee is struggling to meet their goals, offer guidance, training, or resources to help them succeed.

Example: "I've noticed you've been updating your reports more consistently. Great work! Let's meet again in two weeks to discuss any additional support you might need to keep this progress going."

Documenting Performance Conversations

Documenting performance conversations is important for maintaining transparency, setting clear expectations, and tracking progress over time. Documentation serves as a reference point for future discussions and helps ensure consistency.

How to Document a Performance Conversation:

1. **Summarize Key Points:** Write a summary of the main points discussed, including both positive feedback and areas for improvement.

2. **Include Agreed-Upon Goals:** Document the SMART goals or action items agreed upon during the conversation.

3. **Record Follow-Up Steps:** Note any future meetings, deadlines, or additional resources that were discussed.

Example: After a performance conversation, email a summary to the employee, outlining their strengths, areas for improvement, goals, and the next scheduled check-in.

Summary and Key Takeaways

Performance conversations are essential for aligning individual performance with team and organizational goals. By approaching these conversations with empathy, structure, and a collaborative mindset, you create an environment where employees feel supported and motivated to grow.

Key Takeaways:

- **Prepare Thoroughly:** Review relevant data, set clear objectives, and gather specific examples to make the conversation productive and focused.

- **Set a Constructive Tone:** Begin with positive acknowledgments and maintain an empathetic, open-minded approach throughout the conversation.

- **Balance Positive and Corrective Feedback:** Recognize strengths and offer constructive guidance for improvement, using specific examples and neutral language.

- **Set SMART Goals:** Define specific, measurable, achievable, relevant, and time-bound goals to provide clear direction.

- **Encourage Self-Reflection and Collaboration:** Involve the employee in the conversation, allowing them to share their insights and suggest solutions.

- **Follow Up Consistently:** Schedule regular check-ins to track progress, provide additional support, and reinforce positive changes.

- **Document the Conversation:** Keep a record of the main points, goals, and follow-up actions for future reference.

In the next chapter, we'll shift our focus to managing conflicts and interpersonal tensions in the workplace. By combining effective performance conversations with conflict resolution skills, you'll be able to navigate challenging situations with confidence and clarity, fostering a cohesive and productive team environment.

7

MANAGING CONFLICTS
AND INTERPERSONAL TENSIONS

Conflict is a natural part of any workplace, where diverse perspectives, goals, and personalities intersect daily. While conflict can sometimes feel uncomfortable, it doesn't have to be destructive. When managed well, conflict can lead to new ideas, improved communication, and stronger relationships. However, mishandling conflict can result in lasting tension, reduced morale, and a negative impact on productivity.

This chapter explores strategies for managing conflicts and interpersonal tensions in the workplace effectively. We'll discuss techniques for identifying the root causes of conflict, maintaining a calm and neutral stance, encouraging open communication, and finding solutions that satisfy all parties involved. By approaching conflict with empathy and a solution-oriented mindset, you can transform challenging situations into opportunities for growth and collaboration.

Understanding the Nature of Workplace Conflict

Conflict in the workplace can arise from a variety of sources, such as differing communication styles, unclear expectations, workload imbalances, and personality clashes. Recognizing the underlying cause of conflict helps you address the root of the issue rather than just managing surface-level symptoms.

Common Causes of Workplace Conflict:

1. **Miscommunication:** Misunderstandings or unclear communication can easily lead to conflict, especially if information is lacking or misinterpreted.

2. **Differing Work Styles:** People have unique approaches to work—some prefer structure, while others thrive on flexibility. These differences can lead to tension if not managed well.

3. **Competing Goals or Priorities:** Conflicts often arise when team members have competing objectives or feel that their work isn't aligned with team goals.

4. **Personality Differences:** Differences in personality or temperament can create friction if team members don't understand or respect each other's styles.

5. **Resource Constraints:** Limited time, budget, or access to resources can create stress, leading to conflict as people vie for what they need to complete their work.

Example: A common source of conflict is when one team member prefers to communicate through detailed emails, while another prefers quick, verbal updates. This misalignment can cause frustration if both parties feel their preferred style isn't respected.

Recognizing When to Intervene

Not all conflicts require intervention, but it's important to know when stepping in can prevent further escalation. Minor disagreements can often be resolved between the parties involved, while more serious or prolonged conflicts may require managerial or HR intervention to prevent harm to team dynamics and productivity.

Signs That Intervention is Needed:

1. **Ongoing Tension:** If tension persists and affects morale, it may be time to address the issue.

2. **Impact on Performance:** If the conflict is affecting one or both parties' productivity or the overall team's efficiency, intervention can help restore focus.

3. **Escalation of Behavior:** If tempers are flaring or disagreements are becoming personal, the conflict may escalate without support.

4. **Teamwide Disruption:** When a conflict impacts team meetings, project outcomes, or client interactions, it's essential to address it proactively.

Example: If two employees' disagreement over a project timeline repeatedly disrupts team meetings and prevents productive discussion, intervention may be necessary to resolve the issue constructively.

Approaching Conflict with a Solution-Oriented Mindset

The mindset you bring to conflict resolution significantly influences the outcome. By focusing on solutions rather than blame, you create a positive environment for finding common ground. This approach helps prevent defensiveness and encourages both parties to work collaboratively toward a resolution.

Steps for a Solution-Oriented Approach:

1. **Stay Neutral:** Approach the situation without taking sides or assuming one party is right. A neutral stance allows you to mediate effectively and build trust with both parties.

2. **Encourage Both Perspectives:** Give each person the opportunity to share their side without interruption, demonstrating that you value each perspective.

3. **Focus on Common Goals:** Highlight shared objectives that both parties can work toward, such as team productivity, project success, or client satisfaction.

4. **Frame the Discussion Positively:** Use positive language to keep the conversation constructive. Avoid phrases that place blame and focus on words that promote understanding and cooperation.

Example: When mediating a disagreement over workload distribution, emphasize the shared goal of completing the project efficiently and meeting client expectations, rather than focusing on who should have taken more responsibility.

Conflict Resolution with Remote or Distributed Teams

Conflict resolution can be particularly challenging in remote or distributed teams, where communication is often limited to digital channels. Without face-to-face interaction, misunderstandings may escalate quickly, making it essential to approach conflict with intentionality.

Tips for Managing Conflict in Remote Teams:

1. **Address Issues Early:** Don't let misunderstandings fester. If you notice tension in virtual meetings or communication channels, address it directly with a one-on-one or team conversation.

2. **Encourage Video Calls for Important Discussions:** Video calls provide nonverbal cues that can help reduce misunderstandings and build rapport.

3. **Clarify Communication Norms:** Establish norms for respectful communication in digital spaces. Encourage team members to be mindful of their tone in emails or chat messages, where intentions can be easily misinterpreted.

4. **Check In Regularly:** Make regular check-ins a part of your routine to provide opportunities for team members to raise concerns privately if they feel uncomfortable doing so in group settings.

Example: If a conflict arises over differing interpretations of a project deadline in a remote team, schedule a video call to clarify expectations and ensure all parties feel aligned moving forward.

When to Involve HR or Seek Mediation

Some conflicts require additional support, especially if they involve serious issues like harassment, discrimination, or significant breaches of company policy. Knowing when to involve HR or seek mediation helps ensure conflicts are handled professionally and in compliance with company guidelines.

When to Involve HR or a Mediator:

1. **Escalation of Behavior:** If a conflict escalates to include aggressive or unprofessional behavior, HR intervention may be necessary.

2. **Allegations of Harassment or Discrimination:** Any accusations related to harassment or discrimination should be taken seriously and addressed by HR to ensure a fair, impartial process.

3. **Repeated, Unresolved Conflicts:** If conflicts continue despite attempts at resolution, HR can provide additional support or mediation to find a long-term solution.

4. **Legal or Ethical Concerns:** Conflicts involving legal or ethical issues require formal intervention to protect the rights of all parties involved.

Example: If two employees repeatedly clash in a way that disrupts team meetings, despite mediation efforts, HR intervention may be required to assess the situation and recommend a formal resolution.

Documenting Conflict Resolution Efforts

Documenting your conflict resolution efforts helps maintain transparency, accountability, and a clear record of the steps taken to address the issue. This documentation is especially important if the conflict persists or if HR intervention becomes necessary.

Steps for Documenting Conflict Resolution:

1. **Summarize the Issue:** Briefly describe the nature of the conflict and the parties involved.

2. **Outline Resolution Efforts:** Document each step taken to address the conflict, including any meetings, discussions, or adjustments made.

3. **Record Agreements and Next Steps:** Include any agreements

reached, action items, or next steps, as well as a plan for follow-up if needed.

4. **Maintain Confidentiality:** Respect confidentiality by limiting documentation access to relevant parties and keeping personal details private.

Example: After a conflict resolution meeting, email a summary to both parties, outlining the agreed-upon actions, expectations, and follow-up date.

Summary and Key Takeaways

Managing workplace conflict requires patience, empathy, and a structured approach. By identifying the root causes of conflict, fostering open communication, and encouraging collaborative problem-solving, you can transform challenging situations into opportunities for growth.

Key Takeaways:

- **Identify Root Causes:** Understanding the underlying reasons for conflict helps you address the issue effectively.

- **Take a Solution-**Oriented Approach: Focus on finding a solution rather than assigning blame to prevent defensiveness and foster collaboration.

- **Use Conflict Resolution Techniques:** Practice active listening, reframe the conflict, and encourage win-win solutions to keep discussions constructive.

- **Recognize When to Seek Help:** In serious or recurring conflicts, involve HR or consider formal mediation to ensure a fair resolution.

- **Document the Process:** Keep a record of conflict resolution efforts for accountability and reference if further intervention is needed.

In the next chapter, we'll discuss conversations about career growth and development. By combining conflict resolution skills with a focus on personal development, you can create a workplace culture that values growth, respect, and continuous improvement.

8

DISCUSSING CAREER GROWTH
AND DEVELOPMENT

Career growth and development conversations are essential for keeping employees engaged, motivated, and aligned with the organization's goals. When handled well, these discussions provide clarity around career aspirations, identify areas for skill development, and offer support for achieving professional goals. For managers, these conversations are opportunities to deepen relationships with team members, understand their unique motivations, and foster a culture of continuous learning.

This chapter delves into strategies for discussing career development with employees in a way that feels supportive, realistic, and inspiring. We'll cover how to set a positive tone, ask the right questions to uncover an employee's aspirations, set actionable development goals, and address common challenges, such as limited opportunities or mismatched expectations. By the end of this chapter, you'll be equipped to facilitate meaningful career growth conversations that empower your team members and align their ambitions with the organization's objectives.

The Importance of Career Development Conversations

Career development discussions are no longer just an annual exercise;

employees today want ongoing support and clarity regarding their growth potential. These conversations allow managers to address employee needs proactively, improving retention, job satisfaction, and performance.

Benefits of Regular Career Growth Discussions:

1. **Increases Job Satisfaction:** When employees see that their manager is invested in their growth, they feel valued and more satisfied with their role.

2. **Improves Retention:** Employees who feel their development is supported are more likely to stay with the organization.

3. **Enhances Skill Alignment:** Career conversations help identify the skills employees need to develop to advance, allowing managers to align training opportunities with team goals.

4. **Boosts Engagement and Motivation:** Employees are more engaged and motivated when they have clear goals and a sense of purpose within their role.

Example: An employee with a goal of moving into a project management role will feel more motivated and engaged if their manager actively supports their development, such as by offering mentorship or assigning relevant responsibilities.

Preparing for a Career Growth Conversation

Preparation is key to a productive career conversation. Managers should approach these discussions with a clear understanding of the employee's current role, past performance, and potential areas for growth. Preparation also includes being open to new insights the employee may bring to the table about their own aspirations.

Steps for Preparing a Career Growth Conversation:

1. **Review Performance and Feedback:** Reflect on the employee's recent performance, including strengths and areas for development. This context will help guide the conversation.

2. **Consider Development Opportunities:** Think about growth opportunities within the organization and how they might align with the employee's interests and skills.

3. **Be Ready to Listen:** Approach the conversation with an open mind and a willingness to learn about the employee's goals, even if they don't align perfectly with your expectations.

4. **Prepare Resources:** Have information about relevant training programs, mentorship opportunities, or potential project assignments that may support the employee's growth.

Example: Before meeting with an employee who has expressed interest in leadership, review their recent project performance, assess their current skills, and prepare information about leadership development programs within the company.

Setting a Positive and Supportive Tone

The tone you set in a career conversation can significantly impact how comfortable the employee feels sharing their goals. By creating an open, supportive environment, you encourage them to discuss their ambitions honestly and explore possibilities without fear of judgment.

Tips for Setting a Positive Tone:

1. **Express Genuine Interest:** Show that you're genuinely interested in the employee's aspirations by listening attentively and asking thoughtful questions.

2. **Encourage Openness:** Let them know that this is a safe space to discuss both short- and long-term goals, as well as any uncertainties they may have.

3. **Focus on Possibilities:** Approach the conversation with a mindset of exploring possibilities rather than focusing on limitations or obstacles.

4. **Acknowledge Their Efforts and Achievements:** Recognizing their

current contributions sets a positive foundation and makes them feel valued.

Asking Open-Ended Questions to Uncover Aspirations

To understand an employee's true career aspirations, ask open-ended questions that encourage them to reflect on their interests, strengths, and goals. Avoid leading questions that might pressure them to align their goals with what you expect or assume.

Examples of Open-Ended Questions:

1. **"Where do you see yourself in the next few years?"**

2. **"What skills or areas are you most interested in developing?"**

3. **"Are there any projects or roles you've seen within the company that you'd like to learn more about?"**

4. **"What motivates you the most in your work?"**

5. **"Is there anything about your current role that you'd like to change or expand upon?"**

Setting Development Goals with the IDP Framework

An Individual Development Plan (IDP) is a personalized roadmap for achieving career goals and acquiring the skills necessary to advance. IDPs benefit both the employee and the organization by aligning personal aspirations with team or company objectives.

Steps for Creating an Effective IDP:

1. **Define Specific Goals:** Outline what the employee aims to accomplish. This could include new skills, certifications, or specific responsibilities.

2. **Identify Skills and Training Needs:** List the skills they need to acquire to achieve their goals, and identify relevant training or learning opportunities.

3. **Set Milestones and Timeframes**: Break down each goal into smaller, manageable milestones with target completion dates.

Providing Growth Opportunities Within Current Roles

Career development doesn't always require a job change or promotion; many growth opportunities exist within an employee's current role. By offering these opportunities, you can support their development while meeting organizational needs.

Ideas for Growth Within Current Roles:

1. **Project Leadership:** Assign them to lead a project or initiative, allowing them to develop leadership, decision-making, and time management skills.

2. **Cross-Departmental Collaboration:** Encourage them to work with other departments to expand their skill set and gain broader organizational insights.

3. **Skill Development Workshops:** Suggest workshops, webinars, or courses that align with their interests and career goals.

4. **Mentorship and Coaching:** Pair them with a mentor or coach who can provide guidance, insights, and support for their growth.

Addressing Challenges and Managing Expectations

Not all career aspirations can be immediately fulfilled, especially in organizations with limited resources or opportunities. However, it's still possible to support employees' goals while managing expectations and being honest about potential limitations.

Strategies for Managing Expectations:

1. **Be Transparent About Limitations:** If opportunities for promotion or role changes are limited, be honest with the employee while showing support for other development avenues.

2. **Encourage a Long-Term Perspective:** Remind them that career

growth is a long-term journey and that smaller steps now can lead to bigger opportunities later.

3. **Focus on Transferable Skills:** Emphasize skill development that can benefit them regardless of their role. Even if a specific position isn't available, skills like leadership, project management, or communication are valuable in many contexts.

4. **Explore Alternative Paths:** If their initial goal isn't feasible, help them explore alternative paths within the organization that may align with their interests.

Example: If an employee wants to move into a management role but there are no current openings, suggest they take on leadership responsibilities within a project or become a mentor to a junior team member. This helps them develop relevant skills while waiting for an official opportunity.

Encouraging Self-Directed Development

Empowering employees to take charge of their own development encourages independence, motivation, and accountability. Self-directed development may include personal learning goals, industry certifications, or skill-building projects outside of work.

Ways to Encourage Self-Directed Development:

1. **Recommend Online Learning Platforms:** Suggest resources like LinkedIn Learning, Coursera, or industry-specific certifications they can pursue independently.

2. **Encourage Professional Networking:** Support their involvement in professional organizations, conferences, or industry events where they can learn from peers and gain new insights.

3. **Promote Personal Projects:** Encourage employees to work on side projects that align with their career goals, such as learning a new programming language or building a portfolio of work.

4. **Recognize Their Efforts:** Show appreciation for their self-directed

learning initiatives and discuss how these new skills may be applied within their current role.

Example: If an employee is interested in digital marketing, suggest they take an online course in social media strategy and offer opportunities to apply their new skills on relevant projects within the company.

Navigating Difficult Conversations about Career Development

Sometimes, career growth conversations involve difficult topics, such as misaligned goals, lack of advancement opportunities, or performance issues that need to be addressed before considering development. Navigating these conversations with empathy and transparency is essential for maintaining trust and motivation.

Strategies for Difficult Career Conversations:

1. **Acknowledge Their Goals, Even If They're Unachievable Right Now:** Recognize their aspirations and express appreciation for their ambition, even if the specific opportunity isn't currently available.

2. **Be Transparent about Performance Requirements:** If there are performance areas that need improvement, be honest about the steps they need to take before considering a role change or promotion.

3. **Offer Alternative Development Options:** If the desired opportunity isn't feasible, suggest alternative growth paths or projects that align with their interests.

4. **Encourage a Long-Term Perspective:** Help them see how current efforts will benefit their career in the long run, even if they're not immediately advancing to a new role.

Example: If an employee wants to move into a leadership role but needs improvement in communication skills, acknowledge their goal and suggest a public speaking course or mentorship to support their growth in that area.

Summary and Key Takeaways

Career growth conversations are invaluable for fostering a motivated, engaged workforce. By supporting employees in setting realistic goals, developing new skills, and understanding their potential, you contribute to their professional development and strengthen your team's capacity.

Key Takeaways:

- **Prepare for the Conversation:** Review the employee's performance, consider available development opportunities, and be ready to listen to their aspirations.

- **Ask Open-Ended Questions:** Use open-ended questions to understand their goals, motivations, and areas of interest.

- **Set Development Goals with the IDP Framework:** Create a clear Individual Development Plan that outlines skills, milestones, and timelines for growth.

- **Encourage Growth Within Current Roles:** Offer opportunities for development through project leadership, cross-departmental work, and skill-building initiatives.

- **Manage Expectations and Address Challenges:** Be honest about limitations, set realistic expectations, and explore alternative paths when needed.

- **Follow Up Regularly:** Track progress, provide ongoing support, and celebrate achievements to reinforce motivation.

In the next chapter, we'll explore strategies for addressing personal boundaries and mental health concerns in the workplace, a critical aspect of supporting employees in today's work environment. By combining career growth discussions with a commitment to mental well-being, you can create a holistic approach to employee development and satisfaction.

9

ADDRESSING PERSONAL BOUNDARIES AND MENTAL HEALTH CONCERNS

As mental health awareness grows, organizations are recognizing the importance of supporting employees' well-being. Conversations about personal boundaries and mental health concerns are becoming more common and essential for creating a workplace culture that respects each individual's needs and promotes a healthy work-life balance. Addressing these topics can be delicate, as they often touch on deeply personal matters, but when approached with empathy and respect, they strengthen trust and foster a more supportive, productive environment.

In this chapter, we will explore how to navigate discussions around personal boundaries and mental health in a way that respects privacy, offers meaningful support, and aligns with organizational policies. We'll cover techniques for setting and respecting boundaries, strategies for discussing mental health concerns, and guidelines for providing resources while maintaining confidentiality. By the end of this chapter, you'll be better prepared to handle these conversations thoughtfully, creating a workplace culture where employees feel valued and supported.

Understanding the Importance of Boundaries and Mental Health in the Workplace

In a world where work-life boundaries are increasingly blurred, especially with remote and hybrid work arrangements, respecting personal boundaries and supporting mental health is essential. Employees who feel their boundaries are honored and their mental health is valued are more engaged, motivated, and loyal.

Benefits of Supporting Boundaries and Mental Health:

1. **Increases Productivity and Engagement**: Employees who feel respected and supported are more likely to engage actively in their work.

2. **Reduces Burnout and Absenteeism**: Acknowledging and accommodating mental health needs can prevent burnout and reduce the likelihood of prolonged absences.

3. **Fosters Trust and Loyalty**: Employees who feel safe discussing their needs are more likely to remain loyal and committed to the organization.

4. **Promotes a Positive Workplace Culture**: A workplace that prioritizes mental health and boundaries cultivates an atmosphere of mutual respect, compassion, and well-being.

Example: An employee who feels overwhelmed with a heavy workload may be at risk of burnout if their needs aren't recognized. By respecting their boundaries and offering flexibility or support, the organization helps maintain their productivity and morale.

Setting and Respecting Personal Boundaries

Personal boundaries are essential for maintaining a healthy work-life balance, but they can vary greatly from person to person. Some employees may prefer a clear separation between work and personal life, while others may feel comfortable blending the two. Respecting these boundaries is crucial for fostering a sense of security and well-being.

Common Types of Boundaries in the Workplace:

1. **Time Boundaries**: Preferences around work hours, such as avoiding work communications after a certain time.

2. **Task Boundaries**: Preferences for workload management, including the types of tasks or projects an employee is willing to take on.

3. **Emotional Boundaries**: Personal limits around emotional involvement, such as discussing sensitive topics or managing conflict.

4. **Physical Boundaries**: Space preferences, including the desire for personal space in shared work environments or limitations in physical proximity during interactions.

Example: An employee who values time boundaries might prefer to avoid work-related emails after 6 p.m. Respecting this boundary allows them to disconnect from work and recharge, which ultimately benefits both their mental health and productivity.

How to Discuss Personal Boundaries with Empathy

When discussing boundaries, it's important to create a comfortable environment where employees feel they can share their needs without fear of judgment or repercussions. Empathy, active listening, and open-ended questions are essential tools for understanding and respecting their boundaries.

Steps for Discussing Boundaries:

1. **Set a Supportive Tone**: Start the conversation by expressing that your goal is to support their well-being.

2. **Ask Open-Ended Questions**: Encourage them to share any specific needs or preferences regarding their work-life balance.

3. **Listen Without Judgment**: Show respect for their boundaries, even if they differ from your own or from traditional workplace expectations.

4. **Seek Mutually Agreeable Solutions**: Aim to find solutions that respect their boundaries while meeting organizational needs.

Example: If a team member expresses that they're unable to take on additional tasks due to their current workload, acknowledge their boundary by saying, "I appreciate you letting me know. Let's see if we can find ways to balance your workload so that it remains manageable."

Signs of Mental Health Concerns in the Workplace

While managers and colleagues are not responsible for diagnosing mental health conditions, being aware of common signs of distress can help you provide timely support and resources. Subtle changes in behavior, mood, or productivity can sometimes indicate that an employee is struggling.

Common Signs of Mental Health Challenges:

1. **Decreased Productivity**: A noticeable decline in work quality or output, especially if previously consistent.

2. **Frequent Absences**: Uncharacteristic absenteeism or tardiness, which may indicate avoidance or stress.

3. **Withdrawal from Colleagues**: Reduced social engagement or avoidance of team activities.

4. **Visible Fatigue or Irritability**: Changes in demeanor, such as increased irritability or visible signs of exhaustion.

5. **Difficulty Concentrating**: Challenges with focus, attention to detail, or memory.

Example: If an employee who is typically punctual begins arriving late frequently, it could indicate stress, burnout, or other mental health concerns. This may warrant a private conversation to check in on their well-being.

How to Approach Conversations about Mental Health

Initiating a conversation about mental health can feel challenging, as it is a sensitive topic. It's important to approach the conversation with compassion, respect for privacy, and a focus on support rather than diagnosis or judgment.

Guidelines for Approaching Mental Health Conversations:

1. **Choose a Private Setting**: Find a quiet, confidential space where the employee feels safe to speak openly.

2. **Express Genuine Concern**: Begin by expressing your concern about their well-being rather than focusing on productivity or behavior alone.

3. **Use Nonjudgmental Language**: Avoid assumptions or labels. Instead, focus on observations, such as "I've noticed you seem more tired lately" or "I've noticed a change in your usual energy."

4. **Offer Support**: Emphasize that your goal is to provide support and that you're available to discuss ways the organization can help.

5. **Respect Their Privacy**: Recognize that the employee may not want to share details and reassure them that they are not required to disclose personal information.

Example Conversation Starter: "I just wanted to check in and see how you're doing. I've noticed you've seemed a bit stressed lately, and I wanted to see if there's anything I can do to support you. Please know that this is a safe space, and you're not obligated to share anything you're uncomfortable with."

Offering Resources and Support

Organizations often provide resources to support mental health, such as Employee Assistance Programs (EAPs), counseling services, and wellness initiatives. Making employees aware of these resources and encouraging their use can make a significant difference in their well-being.

Ways to Offer Mental Health Support:

1. **Provide Information on Available Resources**: Share details about EAPs, mental health benefits, or on-site counseling services.

2. **Encourage Breaks and Time Off**: Remind employees of their right

to take breaks and personal time if needed, and support them in using this time.

3. **Model Healthy Work-Life Balance**: Lead by example by setting boundaries and promoting self-care practices within the team.

4. **Check In Regularly**: Offer ongoing support through regular check-ins, even after the initial conversation, to ensure they feel supported over time.

Example: "If you ever need a break or some time to regroup, please feel free to let me know. Also, I wanted to remind you about our Employee Assistance Program, which offers free counseling and other resources that may be helpful."

Managing Confidentiality and Privacy

Privacy is critical in discussions about mental health and personal boundaries. Employees need to feel confident that their personal information will be handled with care and discretion. Upholding confidentiality builds trust and encourages employees to seek support without fear of repercussions.

Best Practices for Maintaining Confidentiality:

1. **Limit Information Sharing**: Share only essential information with HR or relevant parties if support or accommodations are required.

2. **Respect Privacy in Team Settings**: Avoid mentioning any personal details in team meetings or shared communication channels.

3. **Store Records Securely**: If documenting the conversation, ensure records are stored securely and are only accessible to those with a legitimate need to know.

4. **Follow Legal and Organizational Guidelines**: Adhere to legal requirements for confidentiality, such as those outlined in health privacy laws, and follow your organization's policies on handling personal information.

Example: If an employee discloses a mental health concern and requests a temporary reduction in workload, communicate only the necessary adjustments to the relevant team members without disclosing the underlying reason.

Supporting Boundaries and Mental Health in Remote and Hybrid Work Environments

Remote and hybrid work arrangements can make it more challenging to identify signs of distress or understand employees' boundaries. Without daily face-to-face interactions, managers need to be intentional about fostering a supportive virtual work environment.

Strategies for Supporting Mental Health and Boundaries Remotely:

1. **Establish Clear Communication Norms**: Set expectations around work hours, response times, and availability to help employees maintain boundaries.

2. **Encourage Regular Breaks**: Remind remote employees to take breaks and maintain a healthy work schedule to prevent burnout.

3. **Check In Consistently**: Schedule regular one-on-one check-ins to discuss their well-being and workload, allowing you to identify any concerns early.

4. **Promote Virtual Wellness Resources**: Share information about virtual wellness programs, online counseling, and other remote-friendly resources.

5. **Be Mindful of Digital Overload**: Avoid excessive virtual meetings or after-hours communications, which can lead to digital fatigue.

Example: In a remote setting, a manager might say, "Please feel free to take regular breaks, and let me know if you're finding the virtual meetings overwhelming. We can explore ways to make the schedule more manageable if needed."

Addressing Resistance to Discussing Boundaries or Mental Health

Not all employees feel comfortable discussing boundaries or mental health concerns, and some may hesitate to share personal information. Respecting their comfort level is essential while offering gentle reminders that support is available.

Tips for Addressing Resistance:

1. **Normalize the Conversation**: Frame discussions about boundaries and mental health as a normal part of workplace well-being to reduce any stigma.

2. **Offer a Confidential Channel**: Provide options for confidential conversations or suggest they reach out to HR if they're more comfortable discussing personal matters privately.

3. **Respect Their Autonomy**: Allow them to share only what they feel comfortable with, without pressuring them to disclose personal details.

4. **Encourage Self-Care**: Even if they're not open to discussing personal challenges, remind them of the importance of self-care and encourage them to take breaks.

Example: If an employee seems resistant, you might say, "I understand if you'd rather keep things private, and that's completely fine. Just know that I'm here to support you, and there are resources available if you ever need them."

Creating a Culture that Values Boundaries and Mental Health

A proactive approach to mental health and personal boundaries fosters a culture of well-being across the organization. By modeling healthy boundaries, providing resources, and encouraging open discussions, managers and leaders can create an environment where employees feel safe and supported.

Ways to Build a Supportive Culture:

1. **Lead by Example**: Model healthy boundaries by setting reasonable work hours, taking breaks, and respecting others' availability.

2. **Integrate Wellness Initiatives**: Promote wellness programs, mental health days, and flexible scheduling as standard practices.

3. **Normalize Mental Health Conversations**: Discuss mental health as a regular part of employee well-being and encourage open, stigma-free conversations.

4. **Provide Training on Mental Health Awareness**: Offer workshops or training sessions that educate employees on mental health, boundary-setting, and support resources.

Example: A manager might openly communicate their own boundary of avoiding after-hours emails, reinforcing to the team that it's acceptable to have work-life boundaries.

Summary and Key Takeaways

Conversations about personal boundaries and mental health are crucial to creating a respectful, supportive, and productive workplace. By approaching these topics with empathy, respect for privacy, and a commitment to providing resources, you create an environment where employees feel safe to prioritize their well-being.

Key Takeaways:

- **Acknowledge the Importance of Boundaries**: Recognize and respect each employee's unique boundaries to foster a healthy work-life balance.

- **Approach Mental Health Conversations with Care**: Use nonjudgmental language, respect privacy, and offer support without pressuring them to disclose personal details.

- **Provide Resources and Support**: Share information about mental health resources, encourage breaks, and model healthy work-life boundaries.

- **Maintain Confidentiality**: Handle personal information with discretion and follow organizational and legal guidelines on privacy.

- **Support Remote Employees' Boundaries**: Set clear communication norms and regularly check in to ensure remote employees feel supported.

In the next chapter, we'll examine communication challenges unique to remote and hybrid work environments, discussing strategies for maintaining connection, clarity, and team cohesion. Combining mental health support with effective remote communication practices allows you to build a resilient, engaged team in today's dynamic work landscape.

10

NAVIGATING REMOTE AND HYBRID WORK COMMUNICATION CHALLENGES

The shift to remote and hybrid work has introduced a new set of communication challenges for teams. Without face-to-face interactions, employees may feel disconnected, miscommunications can escalate, and maintaining team cohesion requires deliberate effort. Clear, empathetic communication is essential in remote and hybrid environments to keep teams aligned, engaged, and productive.

This chapter covers strategies for overcoming the unique obstacles of remote and hybrid work. We'll explore techniques for setting communication norms, building a strong virtual culture, managing digital overload, and fostering inclusivity. By the end of this chapter, you'll be equipped with tools and best practices to support effective communication and collaboration across various work environments.

Understanding the Challenges of Remote and Hybrid Communication

Remote and hybrid work comes with unique communication barriers that can affect team dynamics, productivity, and morale. Understanding these challenges helps you proactively address them and develop strategies for a more cohesive virtual work environment.

Common Communication Challenges in Remote and Hybrid Work:

1. **Lack of Face-to-Face Interaction**: Without in-person meetings, it's harder to interpret nonverbal cues and build rapport, which can lead to misunderstandings.

2. **Isolation and Disconnection**: Remote employees may feel isolated from the rest of the team, affecting their engagement and motivation.

3. **Digital Fatigue**: The increase in virtual meetings, messages, and emails can lead to digital overload and fatigue.

4. **Time Zone Differences**: For distributed teams, scheduling meetings or collaborating in real-time can be challenging.

5. **Unclear Boundaries**: Remote work can blur the boundaries between work and personal life, leading to overworking and burnout if not managed.

Example: A remote employee who doesn't interact frequently with their team might feel left out, impacting their sense of belonging and potentially leading to disengagement over time.

Setting Clear Communication Norms and Expectations

Establishing clear communication norms is essential for maintaining consistency and ensuring that everyone understands when, where, and how to communicate. Well-defined expectations reduce misunderstandings, improve responsiveness, and foster a more organized virtual environment.

Key Elements of Effective Communication Norms:

1. **Define Communication Channels**: Specify which platforms are used for different types of communication, such as email for formal updates, messaging apps for quick questions, and video calls for in-depth discussions.

2. **Set Response Time Expectations**: Establish realistic response times for messages and emails, so employees don't feel pressured to respond immediately to every message.

3. **Clarify Availability**: Encourage team members to set working hours or indicate their availability, especially for teams across multiple time zones.

4. **Schedule Regular Check-Ins**: Regular one-on-ones or team check-ins create a routine and provide opportunities to discuss progress, share updates, and address challenges.

Example: A team might establish a norm that emails will be responded to within 24 hours, while instant messages on platforms like Slack should be answered within a few hours during working hours. This helps employees prioritize their responses and manage their time effectively.

Building and Maintaining a Strong Virtual Team Culture

A strong team culture is critical to keeping remote employees engaged, motivated, and connected. While creating a sense of belonging is more challenging in a virtual setting, it's possible with intentional, consistent efforts to foster camaraderie and trust.

Strategies for Building Virtual Team Culture:

1. **Host Virtual Social Events**: Regular virtual gatherings, such as coffee chats, game nights, or virtual happy hours, can help team members bond and get to know each other outside of work tasks.

2. **Celebrate Milestones and Achievements**: Recognize birthdays, work anniversaries, project completions, or individual achievements in team meetings or on shared platforms to build morale and show appreciation.

3. **Create Shared Traditions**: Develop team traditions, such as themed "remote days" or "Friday Wins" where team members share positive news or accomplishments.

4. **Encourage Personal Connections**: Use icebreakers or set aside time for personal updates at the start of meetings to foster familiarity and build relationships.

Example: A team could start each weekly meeting by having one person share a "fun fact" about themselves or something interesting they learned that week. These small traditions create opportunities for connection in a virtual environment.

Managing Digital Overload and Meeting Fatigue

One of the main challenges in remote work is the risk of digital overload, caused by the constant influx of emails, messages, and virtual meetings. This can lead to burnout, stress, and reduced productivity. Managing communication frequency and prioritizing meaningful interactions can help reduce digital fatigue.

Tips for Managing Digital Overload:

1. **Limit Meeting Frequency**: Evaluate the necessity of each meeting, and consider whether some discussions could be handled via email or messaging.

2. **Introduce "No-Meeting Days"**: Designate specific days without meetings to allow employees uninterrupted time for focused work.

3. **Encourage Shorter Meetings**: Use shorter meeting formats, such as 15- or 30-minute check-ins, to keep discussions efficient and minimize fatigue.

4. **Set Boundaries Around Communication**: Encourage employees to turn off notifications during non-working hours to respect their boundaries and prevent burnout.

Example: A team might implement a "No-Meeting Wednesday" policy, allowing everyone a day free from meetings to concentrate on deep work without interruptions.

Promoting Inclusivity in Remote and Hybrid Teams

Inclusivity can be more challenging to achieve in a remote setting, where certain voices may dominate virtual discussions, or team members in different locations may feel disconnected. Creating an inclusive virtual environment requires deliberate strategies to ensure that everyone has equal opportunities to participate, contribute, and feel valued.

Strategies for Fostering Inclusivity:

1. **Rotate Meeting Times for Global Teams**: For teams across different time zones, alternate meeting times to ensure everyone can participate at a reasonable hour.

2. **Encourage Equal Participation**: Use "round-robin" discussions, where each person shares their thoughts in turn, or invite quieter team members to speak up if they haven't contributed.

3. **Be Mindful of Cultural Sensitivity**: Recognize and respect cultural differences in communication styles and avoid assumptions based on location or background.

4. **Provide Multiple Communication Channels**: Offer different ways for employees to contribute ideas, such as written feedback, anonymous surveys, or post-meeting follow-ups.

Example: In a meeting with participants from various locations, a manager could rotate the meeting start time each month so that no one group is consistently required to join late at night or early in the morning.

Adapting Feedback and Performance Conversations for Remote Teams

Providing feedback in a remote or hybrid setting requires a mindful approach, as it's harder to gauge tone and body language through digital communication. Performance conversations should be approached with clarity, empathy, and an awareness of the challenges unique to remote work.

Best Practices for Virtual Feedback and Performance Discussions:

1. **Use Video for Important Conversations**: For performance

reviews, feedback sessions, or sensitive discussions, use video calls to foster a more personal connection and ensure clearer communication.

2. **Be Direct Yet Supportive**: In written feedback, avoid overly casual language that could be misinterpreted. Instead, be clear and constructive while maintaining a supportive tone.

3. **Acknowledge Remote Work Challenges**: Recognize the unique challenges of remote work, such as isolation or balancing home responsibilities, and factor these into your assessment and feedback.

4. **Provide Regular Check-Ins**: Instead of waiting for formal performance reviews, schedule regular one-on-one check-ins to provide ongoing feedback and keep employees aligned with goals.

Example: During a virtual performance review, a manager might acknowledge that the employee's project timeline was impacted by childcare challenges due to the pandemic. This shows understanding and empathy for remote work realities.

Leveraging Technology for Effective Communication

Technology is a powerful enabler of remote work, but it's essential to use the right tools for different types of communication. Selecting and using technology thoughtfully helps prevent miscommunication and ensures that employees have the tools they need to collaborate effectively.

Recommended Tools for Remote Communication:

1. **Video Conferencing Tools**: Use platforms like Zoom or Microsoft Teams for meetings, team-building sessions, and one-on-ones that require face-to-face interaction.

2. **Instant Messaging Platforms**: Tools like Slack or Microsoft Teams facilitate quick questions and informal updates but should be used with boundaries to avoid constant interruptions.

3. **Project Management Software**: Tools like Asana, Trello, or

Monday.com help teams track progress, assign tasks, and stay organized without requiring constant check-ins.

4. **Collaboration Platforms**: Shared documents and collaborative platforms like Google Workspace or SharePoint make it easy to collaborate on files and maintain version control.

5. **Feedback and Recognition Tools**: Platforms like 15Five or Bonusly allow managers and peers to provide regular feedback and recognition, keeping employees engaged and appreciated.

Example: A team might use Slack for daily check-ins, Zoom for weekly team meetings, and Asana to track project deadlines and deliverables, ensuring everyone is aligned and has access to the information they need.

Building Trust in a Virtual Environment

Trust is foundational to any team's success, and it can be more challenging to build and maintain in a remote setting where casual interactions are limited. Building trust requires intentional actions, such as transparent communication, accountability, and reliability.

Ways to Build Trust Virtually:

1. **Encourage Transparency**: Share team updates, project progress, and challenges openly so everyone feels informed and connected to the organization's goals.

2. **Follow Through on Commitments**: Demonstrate reliability by meeting deadlines, keeping promises, and being responsive to team members' needs.

3. **Promote Accountability**: Encourage a culture where team members take ownership of their tasks and are responsible for their contributions.

4. **Be Authentic and Approachable**: Show vulnerability and empathy, especially when discussing challenges, to humanize remote interactions.

Example: A manager could share a weekly update email summarizing team goals, successes, and challenges, demonstrating transparency and helping remote team members stay informed about the team's overall direction.

Handling Conflicts and Tensions in Remote Teams

Conflicts can arise in any team, but they may be harder to detect and resolve in a remote environment. Without physical cues, misunderstandings can escalate quickly, so it's essential to address tensions proactively and foster open communication.

Steps for Managing Conflict Remotely:

1. **Address Issues Early**: If you notice signs of tension, address them promptly to prevent escalation.

2. **Use Private Channels**: Schedule one-on-one calls to discuss conflicts privately, allowing team members to express concerns openly without fear of judgment.

3. **Promote Active Listening**: Encourage each party to listen actively and summarize the other person's perspective to ensure understanding.

4. **Seek Collaborative Solutions**: Work with both parties to brainstorm solutions that satisfy everyone's needs, focusing on common goals.

Example: If two team members disagree about project priorities, a manager might schedule a private, mediated discussion where each person can express their concerns and work together to find a compromise.

Summary and Key Takeaways

Navigating communication challenges in remote and hybrid work requires flexibility, intentionality, and empathy. By setting clear expectations, fostering inclusivity, and utilizing the right tools, you can create a collaborative virtual environment that supports productivity and connection.

Key Takeaways:

- **Establish Communication Norms**: Define clear expectations for response times, availability, and preferred communication channels to prevent misunderstandings.

- **Build Virtual Team Culture**: Promote team bonding and celebrate milestones to create a sense of belonging in a remote environment.

- **Manage Digital Overload**: Limit meetings, encourage focused work, and set boundaries around communication to reduce digital fatigue.

- **Ensure Inclusivity**: Rotate meeting times, invite participation, and respect cultural differences to make remote work inclusive.

- **Adapt Feedback for Remote Teams**: Provide feedback through video calls, acknowledge remote work challenges, and maintain regular check-ins.

- **Utilize Technology Thoughtfully**: Choose tools that facilitate effective communication and collaboration, without overwhelming employees.

- **Address Conflicts Promptly**: Resolve conflicts early and privately, encouraging open dialogue and collaborative problem-solving.

In the next chapter, we'll explore best practices for managers and leaders, focusing on the skills and strategies needed to foster strong teams, support employee development, and create a culture of open communication and respect. By mastering remote work communication, managers can lead effectively in today's flexible, digital workplace.

11

BEST PRACTICES FOR MANAGERS AND LEADERS

The role of managers and leaders in today's workplace has evolved beyond directing tasks and overseeing performance. Leaders are now expected to be mentors, coaches, and facilitators who support their teams' growth, foster an inclusive culture, and maintain open lines of communication. A successful leader not only drives productivity but also nurtures the well-being, engagement, and development of each team member.

In this chapter, we'll explore essential practices for managers and leaders to cultivate an environment that values open communication, continuous learning, and mutual respect. We'll cover how to lead by example, support team development, provide constructive feedback, and promote inclusivity and well-being. By implementing these practices, managers and leaders can create a positive and productive work environment that empowers employees to reach their full potential.

The Role of Leaders in Shaping Workplace Culture

Managers and leaders have a profound impact on workplace culture. Their actions, words, and attitudes set the tone for how team members interact, collaborate, and approach their work. A positive culture promotes engagement, motivation, and loyalty, while a toxic culture can lead to high turnover, low morale, and burnout.

Ways Leaders Influence Workplace Culture:

1. **Modeling Values and Behaviors:** Leaders demonstrate organizational values through their daily actions and decisions. For example, a leader who emphasizes transparency and honesty encourages their team to communicate openly.

2. **Fostering Psychological Safety:** By creating an environment where employees feel safe to express ideas and concerns without fear of judgment, leaders promote innovation and open dialogue.

3. **Encouraging Growth and Learning:** Leaders who prioritize development and learning inspire their team to continuously improve, take risks, and seek new knowledge.

4. **Promoting Inclusivity and Respect:** Inclusive leaders respect diverse perspectives, which fosters a sense of belonging and encourages each team member to contribute authentically.

Example: A manager who practices humility and admits when they make mistakes models a growth mindset. This encourages the team to view setbacks as learning opportunities rather than failures.

Leading by Example: Modeling the Behavior You Want to See

Effective leadership begins with leading by example. When managers and leaders embody the qualities they want to instill in their team, it sets a powerful standard. Employees are more likely to adopt behaviors that they see demonstrated by their leaders consistently.

Key Behaviors to Model as a Leader:

1. **Accountability:** Take responsibility for your actions, admit mistakes, and learn from them. Accountability builds trust and sets a standard of integrity.

2. **Respect and Empathy:** Treat every team member with respect and empathy, regardless of their role or background.

3. **Effective Communication:** Communicate openly and clearly,

listen actively, and provide thoughtful responses.

4. **Commitment to Excellence:** Show dedication to high standards and continuous improvement, encouraging others to strive for excellence.

5. **Work-Life Balance:** Model a balanced approach to work, respecting boundaries and prioritizing well-being. This shows your team that it's okay to take breaks and maintain a healthy balance.

Example: A manager who consistently respects their own boundaries by disconnecting after work hours and encouraging team members to do the same sends a message that work-life balance is valued in the organization.

Building Trust and Psychological Safety

Trust and psychological safety are fundamental for a high-performing team. When team members feel safe to voice their opinions, ask questions, and take risks, they are more likely to collaborate effectively, innovate, and work with confidence.

Strategies for Building Trust and Psychological Safety:

1. **Encourage Open Dialogue:** Create opportunities for team members to share their thoughts and feedback in a nonjudgmental setting, such as team meetings or one-on-ones.

2. **Be Transparent:** Share information openly and communicate the reasoning behind decisions. Transparency reduces uncertainty and builds trust.

3. **Address Mistakes with Empathy:** When mistakes occur, approach them with empathy and a focus on solutions rather than blame. This shows that setbacks are part of the learning process.

4. **Invite Diverse Perspectives:** Encourage input from all team members, especially those who may be quieter or less confident. Make it clear that every voice is valued.

Example: A leader might start each team meeting by inviting everyone to share their perspective on ongoing projects. This signals that input from all levels is valued and encourages team members to speak up.

Supporting Team Development and Growth

A major responsibility of leaders is to support their team members' professional growth. When employees see that their managers are invested in their development, they feel more motivated, engaged, and aligned with the organization's goals.

Ways to Support Team Development:

1. **Create Development Plans:** Collaborate with each team member to establish Individual Development Plans (IDPs) that align with their career goals and the organization's needs.

2. **Provide Access to Training and Resources:** Encourage team members to pursue training, certifications, or courses that support their growth. Allocate budget or resources to help them access these opportunities.

3. **Offer Mentorship and Coaching:** Act as a mentor or coach, providing guidance and insights based on your own experience. This can be formal or informal and helps employees develop skills and confidence.

4. **Encourage Stretch Assignments:** Assign tasks or projects that challenge team members and push them out of their comfort zones. Stretch assignments promote skill development and prepare employees for new roles.

Example: A manager might work with an aspiring leader on the team to develop a customized plan that includes shadowing senior managers, leading small projects, and attending leadership workshops.

Providing Regular, Constructive Feedback

Feedback is essential for growth and improvement, but it must be delivered in a way that feels constructive, supportive, and actionable.

Leaders who provide regular feedback create a culture of continuous improvement, where team members feel empowered to learn and develop.

Best Practices for Constructive Feedback:

1. **Use Specific Examples:** Provide specific examples to make feedback clear and actionable. Avoid generalities that may be hard for the employee to interpret.

2. **Balance Positive and Constructive Feedback:** Start with positive feedback to recognize strengths, then provide constructive feedback that focuses on growth areas.

3. **Use the SBI Model:** The Situation-Behavior-Impact model helps keep feedback objective and focused on behaviors rather than personal traits.

4. **Encourage Self-Reflection:** Ask team members to reflect on their performance and self-assess their strengths and areas for improvement.

Example: Instead of saying, "Your presentation was confusing," a leader could say, "In yesterday's presentation (situation), I noticed that the information was a bit dense (behavior), which made it hard for the audience to follow along (impact). Let's work together on simplifying the slides to make the key points more accessible."

Promoting Inclusivity and Diversity

An inclusive leader values and respects diverse perspectives, recognizing that a diverse team brings a wealth of ideas, creativity, and innovation. Promoting inclusivity is not only ethical but also essential for a healthy, productive team culture.

Strategies for Promoting Inclusivity:

1. **Celebrate Diversity:** Recognize and celebrate cultural, linguistic, and personal differences within your team, such as by marking international holidays or hosting cultural events.

2. **Encourage Equal Participation:** Create space for everyone to contribute by inviting input from all team members, especially those who may be quieter in group settings.

3. **Avoid Assumptions:** Be mindful of assumptions based on backgrounds or identities. Treat each team member as an individual with unique skills and perspectives.

4. **Provide Equal Opportunities:** Ensure that growth and advancement opportunities are accessible to all team members, regardless of background.

Example: In a team meeting, a leader might say, "I'd love to hear everyone's ideas on this project. If you haven't had a chance to share, please feel free to jump in." This invitation encourages more inclusive participation.

Supporting Employee Well-Being and Work-Life Balance

Leaders play a crucial role in fostering a healthy work-life balance and supporting employees' well-being. When employees feel their well-being is valued, they are more likely to remain engaged, motivated, and productive.

Ways to Support Well-Being and Balance:

1. **Set Realistic Workload Expectations:** Avoid overloading team members and be mindful of deadlines. Encourage employees to prioritize tasks and seek help if they're overwhelmed.

2. **Respect Boundaries:** Encourage team members to set boundaries, such as not working late or over weekends, and model these boundaries yourself.

3. **Encourage Regular Breaks:** Promote the importance of taking breaks during the day, especially for remote employees who may feel pressure to stay online constantly.

4. **Offer Mental Health Resources:** Make team members aware of any mental health resources available through the organization,

such as Employee Assistance Programs (EAPs) or wellness programs.

Example: A manager might remind their team to disconnect at the end of the day, saying, "Please remember to log off by 6 p.m. and enjoy your evening. Your well-being is important, and I want everyone to have a chance to recharge."

Fostering Open Communication and Transparency

Open communication and transparency are essential for building trust and aligning the team with organizational goals. Leaders who communicate openly with their teams foster a culture of honesty, trust, and mutual respect.

Practices for Transparent Communication:

1. **Share Organizational Updates:** Regularly update the team on important company developments, project statuses, and any changes that may affect their work.

2. **Explain Decisions:** When making decisions, explain the rationale so that team members understand the context and feel included.

3. **Encourage Questions and Feedback:** Make it clear that questions and feedback are welcome. This openness encourages team members to seek clarification rather than making assumptions.

4. **Hold Regular Team Meetings:** Consistent team meetings create opportunities for open communication, collaboration, and alignment on shared goals.

Example: A leader might begin a meeting by saying, "I want to keep you all informed about some upcoming changes to our department structure. Here's what's happening and why. Please feel free to ask questions at any point."

Handling Difficult Conversations with Empathy and Respect

Leaders often need to have difficult conversations about performance, conflicts, or organizational changes. When these conversations are approached with empathy and respect, they strengthen relationships and foster a more supportive work environment.

Strategies for Handling Difficult Conversations:

1. **Prepare Carefully:** Gather relevant information, define your objectives, and plan how you'll approach the conversation.

2. **Choose a Private Setting:** Find a confidential, distraction-free space for sensitive discussions to ensure that the employee feels comfortable.

3. **Use Nonjudgmental Language:** Focus on behaviors or facts, not personal traits, to keep the conversation constructive and respectful.

4. **Listen Actively:** Give the employee a chance to share their perspective, listening without interruption or judgment.

Example: If an employee is underperforming, a leader might say, "I've noticed that you've been having difficulty meeting some of your deadlines. Let's discuss what challenges you're facing and how I can support you in achieving your goals."

Building a Culture of Continuous Improvement and Innovation

Encouraging a culture of continuous improvement and innovation keeps the team adaptable and forward-thinking. Leaders who promote innovation inspire their teams to seek new solutions, learn from mistakes, and continuously enhance their skills.

Ways to Foster Continuous Improvement:

1. **Celebrate Experimentation:** Encourage team members to try new approaches and take calculated risks, even if they don't always lead to success.

2. **Learn from Setbacks:** Treat mistakes as learning opportunities.

Discuss what went wrong, what was learned, and how to improve moving forward.

3. **Encourage Skill-Building:** Support ongoing training and skill development, such as by providing access to courses, workshops, or industry events.

4. **Reward Initiative:** Recognize and reward team members who take the initiative to improve processes, suggest new ideas, or solve problems creatively.

Example: A leader could encourage innovation by saying, "If you have ideas on how we can improve our processes or try something new, please bring them forward. I'd love to hear any creative solutions you have in mind."

Summary and Key Takeaways

Effective leadership requires a balance of empathy, accountability, and commitment to growth. By fostering open communication, supporting development, and prioritizing well-being, leaders create an environment where employees feel valued, engaged, and motivated to contribute their best.

Key Takeaways:

- **Lead by Example:** Model the behaviors and values you want to see in your team, from accountability to work-life balance.

- **Build Trust and Psychological Safety:** Encourage open dialogue, invite diverse perspectives, and support risk-taking without fear of judgment.

- **Support Team Development:** Create development plans, provide mentorship, and encourage stretch assignments to foster continuous growth.

- **Promote Inclusivity and Respect:** Ensure that every team member feels valued, respected, and included in team activities and decision-making.

- **Prioritize Well-Being and Balance:** Set realistic workload expectations, respect boundaries, and offer resources that support mental health and well-being.

- **Handle Difficult Conversations with Empathy:** Approach sensitive topics with preparation, nonjudgmental language, and active listening.

- **Encourage Continuous Improvement:** Foster a culture of learning, innovation, and resilience, where team members feel empowered to take initiative and learn from setbacks.

In the final chapter, we'll look at ways to build a sustainable culture of open communication, inclusivity, and respect, focusing on how these values create a strong foundation for long-term success. By mastering these leadership practices, you're creating a workplace where everyone has the support and opportunity to thrive.

12

MOVING FORWARD: BUILDING A CULTURE OF OPEN COMMUNICATION

Creating a sustainable culture of open communication, inclusivity, and respect requires ongoing effort, intentional strategies, and commitment from every level of the organization. A strong culture is not built overnight but rather through consistent practices, values, and behaviors that reinforce a positive work environment. Leaders play a vital role in shaping this culture, but it's ultimately the responsibility of the entire team to cultivate and maintain these values.

This final chapter explores how to embed open communication, inclusivity, and respect into the organizational DNA. We'll cover strategies for promoting continuous feedback, recognizing contributions, fostering diversity, and supporting well-being. We'll also discuss how to measure cultural progress and adjust strategies over time. By implementing these practices, you create a workplace where employees feel valued, engaged, and empowered, laying the foundation for long-term success and growth.

Embedding Open Communication into the Workplace Culture

Open communication is the cornerstone of a positive workplace culture. When employees feel encouraged to share ideas, voice concerns, and offer feedback, it fosters transparency, trust, and collaboration. Embedding open communication into the culture requires consistent practices and structures that reinforce its value.

Strategies to Foster Open Communication:

1. **Create Feedback Loops:** Implement regular feedback mechanisms, such as surveys, suggestion boxes, and one-on-one meetings, to ensure employees have multiple channels to share their thoughts.

2. **Promote Transparent Decision-Making:** Share the reasoning behind decisions, whether they're related to projects, promotions, or organizational changes. This transparency builds trust and helps employees feel informed.

3. **Encourage Questions and Dialogue:** In team meetings, invite questions and discussions to ensure everyone feels comfortable speaking up. Make it clear that no question is "too small" or "off-limits."

4. **Provide Training in Effective Communication:** Offer training on communication skills, such as active listening, nonverbal cues, and constructive feedback, to empower employees to communicate effectively and confidently.

Example: An organization might hold monthly "Ask Me Anything" (AMA) sessions, where employees can ask senior leaders questions about the company's direction, projects, or policies. This practice encourages transparency and gives employees a voice in the organization.

Encouraging Continuous Feedback and Learning

A culture that values continuous feedback and learning ensures that employees are always growing, improving, and evolving with the organization. Feedback should be a routine part of communication, not something that only happens during formal reviews.

Best Practices for Continuous Feedback and Learning:

1. **Normalize Feedback in Day-to-Day Interactions**

2. **Offer Learning Opportunities**

3. **Encourage Self-Reflection**

4. **Implement Peer Feedback**

Example: A company might establish a "Feedback Friday" tradition, where employees share feedback and recognition for each other's work at the end of each week. This creates a rhythm of continuous improvement and appreciation.

Recognizing and Celebrating Contributions

Recognition is a powerful tool for reinforcing a positive culture. When employees feel that their contributions are valued, they're more likely to stay motivated, engaged, and committed to the organization's mission. Recognition also fosters a sense of belonging and appreciation, which contributes to overall job satisfaction.

Ways to Recognize and Celebrate Contributions:

1. **Implement a Recognition Program:** Establish a formal recognition program that allows employees to recognize each other's efforts, such as a "Peer-to-Peer Kudos" program or monthly awards.

2. **Celebrate Milestones:** Recognize work anniversaries, project completions, and personal achievements, such as earning certifications or completing training.

3. **Highlight Success Stories:** Share success stories and achievements in team meetings or internal newsletters to showcase individual and team contributions.

4. **Practice Public Appreciation:** Encourage managers to recognize accomplishments publicly, whether during meetings, in group emails, or on internal platforms.

Example: A manager might start each team meeting by

acknowledging recent achievements or hard work, such as completing a challenging project or going above and beyond to help a client. This small act of recognition reinforces positive behaviors and contributions.

Fostering Inclusivity and Diversity

An inclusive culture welcomes and values every employee's unique perspectives, backgrounds, and experiences. Diversity enriches teams, boosts creativity, and drives innovation, while inclusivity ensures that everyone feels respected and valued, regardless of their identity or background.

Strategies for Promoting Inclusivity and Diversity:

1. **Establish Inclusive Policies:** Create policies that promote diversity, equity, and inclusion, covering areas such as hiring, career advancement, and anti-discrimination practices.

2. **Encourage Diverse Voices:** Invite employees from diverse backgrounds to participate in decision-making processes and provide a platform for them to share their ideas and perspectives.

3. **Celebrate Cultural Events:** Recognize and celebrate cultural and religious events that are significant to team members, fostering a culture of understanding and respect.

4. **Provide Diversity and Inclusion Training:** Offer workshops on unconscious bias, cultural competence, and inclusive communication to educate and empower employees.

Example: An organization might host monthly "Diversity Dialogues," where team members can discuss topics related to diversity and inclusion in a safe, moderated setting. This fosters awareness and encourages learning about different perspectives.

Supporting Employee Well-Being and Mental Health

Employee well-being and mental health are foundational to a productive and positive workplace. When employees feel supported in maintaining a healthy work-life balance and have access to mental health resources, they're better able to engage in their work and contribute to the team.

Strategies for Supporting Well-Being and Mental Health:

1. **Offer Mental Health Resources:** Provide access to resources such as Employee Assistance Programs (EAPs), counseling services, and mental health days.

2. **Promote Work-Life Balance:** Encourage employees to set boundaries around work hours, take regular breaks, and disconnect during non-working hours.

3. **Create a Culture of Openness Around Mental Health:** Normalize discussions about mental health by openly addressing it in team meetings, newsletters, or wellness programs.

4. **Encourage Use of Paid Time Off:** Encourage employees to take advantage of their vacation and sick leave to recharge and prioritize their well-being.

Example: A company might implement "Wellness Wednesdays," where team members are encouraged to take a longer break for self-care or join a group wellness activity like a yoga session. This demonstrates a commitment to holistic well-being.

Measuring and Tracking Cultural Progress

Creating a sustainable culture requires regular assessment and adjustment. By measuring cultural progress, organizations can identify areas for improvement, track the effectiveness of initiatives, and ensure that they're on the right path toward fostering an inclusive, respectful, and communicative environment.

Methods for Measuring Cultural Progress:

1. **Conduct Employee Surveys:** Use regular surveys to gather employee feedback on workplace culture, inclusivity, communication, and well-being.

2. **Analyze Turnover and Retention Rates:** High retention rates and

low turnover can be indicators of a positive culture, while spikes in turnover may signal areas that need attention.

3. **Hold Focus Groups and Listening Sessions:** Organize focus groups or listening sessions to gather in-depth feedback on cultural initiatives and employee experiences.

4. **Use Key Performance Indicators (KPIs):** Track specific metrics related to engagement, participation in cultural programs, and feedback scores to monitor cultural health.

Example: A company might send quarterly "pulse" surveys with questions about inclusivity, communication effectiveness, and work-life balance. These surveys provide data on how employees feel about the culture and help identify areas for improvement.

Adjusting Strategies Based on Feedback

A sustainable culture requires flexibility and responsiveness. As the organization grows and evolves, leaders need to be open to adapting strategies to address changing needs, feedback, or new challenges. By actively responding to employee input, leaders demonstrate a commitment to continuous improvement.

Steps for Adjusting Cultural Strategies:

1. **Analyze Feedback for Patterns**

2. **Pilot New Initiatives**

3. **Communicate Changes Transparently**

4. **Evaluate the Impact of Changes**

Example: If employees express a desire for more flexibility in work hours, an organization might pilot a flexible schedule option within one department to assess its impact before expanding it to the entire company.

Building Leadership Commitment to Culture

For cultural initiatives to be effective and sustainable, they must have buy-in from leaders at all levels. When leadership is fully committed to open communication, inclusivity, and respect, these values are more likely to be embraced across the organization.

Ways to Ensure Leadership Commitment:

1. **Incorporate Culture into Leadership Development**

2. **Hold Leaders Accountable for Goals**

3. **Recognize and Reward Culture Champions**

4. **Encourage Leaders to Model Culture**

Example: A company might establish "culture KPIs" for managers, including metrics related to team engagement, inclusivity, and employee feedback scores. Leaders who meet or exceed these targets could receive recognition or rewards.

Summary and Key Takeaways

A sustainable culture of open communication, inclusivity, and respect is a continuous journey that requires dedication, transparency, and adaptability. By embedding these values into the core of the organization, leaders create an environment where employees feel valued, engaged, and motivated to contribute their best.

Key Takeaways:

- **Prioritize Open Communication**

- **Foster a Culture of Learning**

- **Recognize Contributions Regularly**

- **Promote Inclusivity and Diversity**

- **Support Well-Being and Work-Life Balance**

- **Measure and Adjust Strategies**

- **Ensure Leadership Commitment**

By following these principles, organizations can build a lasting culture that not only supports business goals but also fosters a fulfilling and inclusive workplace for every team member. In doing so, they create a resilient foundation for future success, where each employee feels empowered, connected, and valued.

CONCLUSION

The Journey Toward a Thriving Workplace Culture

Building and sustaining a workplace culture that values open communication, inclusivity, and respect is not a one-time task; it's an ongoing journey that evolves alongside the organization and its people. A thriving workplace culture is the result of intentional effort, consistent leadership, and a commitment from every individual within the organization. When these values are deeply embedded into daily interactions, decision-making, and company practices, they create a foundation where employees can flourish and bring their best selves to work.

In this conclusion, we'll revisit the core principles that contribute to a healthy workplace culture, reflect on the benefits of fostering such an environment, and explore practical steps for sustaining these values over time. Ultimately, the journey to a positive workplace culture requires dedication, adaptability, and a shared commitment to the growth and well-being of every team member.

Revisiting the Core Principles

Throughout this book, we've explored various strategies for addressing difficult conversations, providing constructive feedback, supporting team development, fostering inclusivity, and promoting well-being. These core principles are interconnected, each reinforcing the other to create a cohesive, supportive workplace culture. Here's a recap of the foundational principles:

1. **Open Communication**: Communication is the backbone of any successful organization. By fostering a culture of openness and transparency, you enable employees to express themselves freely, share ideas, and address challenges constructively. This communication builds trust and facilitates collaboration.

2. **Continuous Feedback and Learning**: A feedback-friendly culture encourages personal and professional growth. By normalizing feedback, both positive and constructive, employees are motivated to improve, learn from mistakes, and reach their full potential. Ongoing learning opportunities reinforce the value of growth and adaptability.

3. **Inclusivity and Respect**: Inclusivity isn't just a policy—it's a way of ensuring that every team member feels valued and appreciated. When diverse voices are welcomed, respected, and heard, the workplace becomes a richer, more creative, and more resilient environment.

4. **Empathy and Support for Well-Being**: Supporting employees' well-being, mental health, and work-life balance is crucial to sustaining engagement and motivation. Leaders who show empathy and provide resources for well-being contribute to a culture where employees feel cared for and valued beyond their output.

5. **Commitment to Growth and Innovation**: A culture that encourages continuous improvement and innovation keeps employees engaged and motivated. By celebrating experimentation, learning from setbacks, and supporting skill-building, organizations empower employees to think creatively and embrace change.

The Benefits of a Positive Workplace Culture

The effort to build and maintain a positive workplace culture yields numerous benefits, both for individual employees and for the organization as a whole. Here are some key benefits of fostering a healthy, inclusive, and communicative work environment:

1. **Higher Employee Engagement**: When employees feel valued, respected, and supported, they are more likely to be engaged and enthusiastic about their work. Engaged employees are often more productive, motivated, and committed to the organization's success.

2. **Reduced Turnover and Greater Retention**: A positive culture encourages loyalty. Employees who feel respected and see opportunities for growth are less likely to leave, resulting in lower turnover rates, reduced hiring costs, and greater retention of institutional knowledge.

3. **Increased Innovation and Creativity**: Diversity and inclusivity encourage the sharing of unique perspectives, leading to more creative problem-solving and innovation. Employees are more willing to take risks and experiment when they feel psychologically safe and supported.

4. **Improved Mental Health and Well-Being**: A culture that prioritizes mental health and well-being allows employees to maintain a healthier work-life balance, reducing stress, burnout, and absenteeism. Employees who feel supported in this way are more likely to bring their best selves to work each day.

5. **Enhanced Reputation and Employer Brand**: A strong, positive culture enhances the organization's reputation, making it a more attractive place to work. Organizations known for their inclusivity, open communication, and respect for employees' well-being often attract top talent and gain a competitive edge in their industry.

Sustaining Cultural Values Over Time

Building a strong culture is one achievement, but maintaining it over time requires dedication, flexibility, and regular reinforcement. As the organization grows and changes, leaders must remain vigilant and responsive, continually assessing cultural health and adapting to new challenges.

Strategies for Sustaining a Positive Culture:

1. **Regularly Assess Culture Health**: Conduct employee surveys, hold feedback sessions, and assess engagement metrics to measure cultural health. Use this feedback to identify areas that may need adjustment or reinforcement.

2. **Celebrate Cultural Milestones**: Recognize and celebrate cultural achievements, such as hitting diversity goals, implementing new well-being initiatives, or increasing feedback participation. Celebrating these milestones reinforces their importance.

3. **Adapt to Organizational Changes**: As the company grows or undergoes transitions, such as mergers or leadership changes, re-evaluate cultural practices to ensure they remain relevant. Stay open to modifying strategies to address new challenges or opportunities.

4. **Embed Culture into Onboarding**: Integrate core cultural values into the onboarding process to ensure that new hires understand and embrace the organization's principles from day one. This approach reinforces culture as a shared responsibility.

5. **Involve Employees in Culture Initiatives**: Give employees a voice in cultural initiatives by inviting them to join committees, participate in decision-making, or suggest improvements. When employees actively shape the culture, they feel a stronger connection to it.

A Call to Action for Leaders and Employees Alike

Creating a sustainable culture of open communication, inclusivity, and respect requires the commitment of leaders and employees at every level. Leaders set the tone by modeling behaviors, reinforcing values, and ensuring that the organization's policies support a positive environment. Employees contribute by engaging actively, respecting each other's perspectives, and upholding the cultural values in their day-to-day interactions.

As you work toward building a stronger culture, remember that everyone plays a role in fostering a supportive and collaborative environment. Small actions—such as offering feedback, recognizing a colleague's contributions, or reaching out to support someone struggling—make a significant difference in creating a workplace where everyone feels valued.

Looking Toward the Future

The journey toward a thriving workplace culture is ongoing. As work environments continue to evolve, influenced by factors like remote work, technological advancements, and changing societal expectations, organizations will need to stay adaptable and innovative. Maintaining open lines of communication, prioritizing inclusivity, and valuing employees' well-being will be as important as ever.

Ultimately, a strong workplace culture is one that grows and adapts alongside the organization. By embracing these principles, you're not only building a culture for today's challenges but also creating a foundation that can sustain your organization through future changes.

Final Thought

The effort to create a positive workplace culture is an investment in the success and well-being of your employees and the organization. It's an ongoing commitment that yields meaningful, lasting benefits. By championing a culture of open communication, inclusivity, and respect, you're building a place where everyone can contribute, grow, and succeed—together.

RESOURCES FOR FURTHER LEARNING AND IMPLEMENTATION

The following resources provide tools, frameworks, and insights for implementing the practices discussed in this book. Whether you're looking to deepen your knowledge on leadership, feedback, mental health support, or inclusivity, these resources offer a wealth of information to support your journey.

1. Books on Leadership, Communication, and Culture

- **Dare to Lead** by Brené Brown: This book explores the power of vulnerability and courage in leadership, offering insights on creating a culture of trust and openness.

- **Radical Candor** by Kim Scott: A practical guide on how to give honest feedback and build strong relationships with colleagues, this book emphasizes the importance of direct communication with empathy.

- **Crucial Conversations: Tools for Talking When Stakes Are High** by Kerry Patterson, Joseph Grenny, Ron McMillan, and Al Switzler: A foundational book on navigating difficult conversations with skill, even when emotions are high.

- **The Culture Code** by Daniel Coyle: Coyle explores the building blocks of strong team cultures, with real-world examples of successful teams and practical tips on fostering belonging and trust.

- **Leaders Eat Last** by Simon Sinek: This book highlights how leaders can create an environment of safety and support, fostering a culture of loyalty and mutual respect.

2. Online Courses and Workshops

- **Coursera – Positive Psychology Specialization** (University of Pennsylvania): This course explores the science behind well-being, resilience, and happiness, offering insights on promoting mental health in the workplace.

- **LinkedIn Learning – Leadership Foundations**: A foundational course on leadership skills, including effective communication, decision-making, and team-building techniques.

- **Udemy – Diversity and Inclusion in the Workplace**: This course provides practical steps for fostering an inclusive work environment, understanding unconscious bias, and promoting diversity.

- **Harvard Online – Negotiation Mastery**: Learn strategies for handling negotiations and difficult conversations with an emphasis on achieving win-win outcomes.

- **MIT Sloan Executive Education – Leading Organizational Change**: This course offers strategies for creating and sustaining a positive culture during periods of change, focusing on adaptability and resilience.

3. Mental Health and Well-Being Resources

- **Employee Assistance Programs (EAPs)**: Many organizations offer EAPs, which provide confidential counseling and mental health support for employees. Check with your HR department to learn more about available resources.

- **Headspace for Work**: Headspace offers mindfulness and meditation tools specifically designed for the workplace, promoting mental well-being and stress reduction.

- **Mind Share Partners**: A nonprofit organization focused on transforming workplace mental health, Mind Share Partners offers training, workshops, and resources for supporting employees' mental health.

- **Mental Health America – Workplace Mental Health**: Mental Health America provides resources, articles, and tools specifically tailored to support mental health in the workplace, including strategies for managers and leaders.

- **Calm for Business**: Calm offers relaxation, sleep, and mindfulness resources for organizations, helping employees manage stress and improve focus.

4. Diversity, Equity, and Inclusion (DEI) Resources

- **Catalyst**: Catalyst offers a variety of resources on creating inclusive workplaces, particularly around gender equity and diversity. They provide research, articles, and toolkits to support DEI efforts.

- **The NeuroLeadership Institute**: This organization focuses on brain-based approaches to DEI, providing insights on unconscious bias, inclusion, and belonging.

- **Project Include**: Project Include provides actionable recommendations for implementing diversity and inclusion strategies, particularly within tech organizations.

- **Better Allies** by Karen Catlin: This book is a practical guide for creating a more inclusive workplace and supporting diversity through everyday actions.

- **The Harvard Business Review Guide to Managing Diversity**: A comprehensive guide for managers on supporting and leveraging diversity within teams, including practical advice and case studies.

5. Feedback and Communication Tools

- **15Five**: A continuous performance management platform that facilitates weekly check-ins, feedback, and goal setting to keep employees aligned and engaged.

- **CultureAmp**: An employee engagement and performance tool that includes feedback, development, and employee survey capabilities to measure and improve workplace culture.

- **SurveyMonkey**: A versatile tool for conducting employee engagement surveys, feedback surveys, and pulse checks to gather insights into workplace culture and communication effectiveness.

- **Officevibe**: An employee engagement tool that provides anonymous feedback options, pulse surveys, and actionable insights on employee satisfaction and well-being.

- **Slack**: Slack facilitates open communication, making it easy for teams to collaborate in real-time. It's useful for keeping communication channels clear and organized, especially in remote and hybrid environments.

6. Key Articles and Reports

- **McKinsey & Company – "The Case for Inclusive Leadership"**: This article explores why inclusivity is essential in today's workplace and provides insights on building inclusive leadership.

- **Deloitte Insights – "The Workforce Ecosystem"**: Deloitte's report explores how to create an agile, resilient workplace that fosters innovation and inclusivity.

- **Gallup – "State of the American Workplace"**: This report provides insights on employee engagement, well-being, and organizational culture, along with strategies for fostering a positive environment.

- **The Society for Human Resource Management (SHRM) – "Creating a Culture That Values Diversity and Inclusion"**: SHRM offers comprehensive resources for implementing DEI strategies, managing conflict, and building an inclusive workplace.

- **Harvard Business Review – "What Great Managers Do Differently"**: This article examines effective management practices and how great managers create a positive and productive culture.

7. Organizations and Associations for Continued Learning

- **Society for Human Resource Management (SHRM)**: SHRM offers a wealth of resources on HR best practices, including culture, engagement, and mental health. They also provide certifications for HR professionals.

- **The NeuroLeadership Institute**: This research-driven institute offers insights on leadership, communication, and DEI with a focus on neuroscience.

- **The Center for Creative Leadership (CCL)**: CCL provides leadership training, research, and development resources, including courses on inclusive leadership, change management, and conflict resolution.

- **Association for Talent Development (ATD)**: ATD offers resources, training, and certifications on learning and development, including courses on building positive workplace culture.

- **BetterUp**: A coaching and training platform for leadership and development, BetterUp focuses on personal growth, resilience, and building a supportive workplace environment.

8. Podcasts on Leadership, Culture, and Mental Health

- **WorkLife with Adam Grant**: Organizational psychologist Adam Grant explores the science of workplace dynamics, culture, and motivation, providing research-based insights and practical advice.

- **The Happiness Lab with Dr. Laurie Santos**: Dr. Laurie Santos shares science-backed strategies for increasing happiness and well-being, both in and out of the workplace.

- **Dare to Lead with Brené Brown**: Brené Brown's podcast focuses on leadership, vulnerability, and creating a culture of trust and openness.

- **HBR IdeaCast**: Hosted by Harvard Business Review, this podcast covers a wide range of topics relevant to workplace culture, leadership, and mental health.

- **The Diversity Gap**: This podcast addresses the challenges of bridging diversity gaps in the workplace, exploring topics like inclusive leadership, equity, and cultural competency.

9. Websites and Blogs for Ongoing Learning

- **Harvard Business Review (HBR)**: HBR provides research-based articles on leadership, communication, DEI, and organizational culture. It's a great resource for staying current on workplace trends.

- **Inc.com**: Inc. offers articles on business leadership, team dynamics, and culture, providing advice for leaders at all levels.

- **MindTools**: This site offers resources and toolkits on personal and professional development, including communication, feedback, and team management skills.

- **The Muse**: The Muse provides career advice and articles focused on workplace culture, inclusivity, and well-being.

- **Medium – "The Startup" and "Leadership" Sections**: Medium features insightful articles on leadership, culture, and communication from industry professionals and thought leaders.

Final Note on Using These Resources

Remember, culture is dynamic. It grows and evolves with every conversation, every feedback session, and every action taken to support inclusivity, respect, and open communication. By leveraging these resources and staying committed to these principles, you're investing in the long-term well-being and success of both your employees and the organization as a whole.

Authors and Influential Works

1. **Brené Brown** – *Dare to Lead*: Focuses on vulnerability, courage, and building trust in leadership, which are key for creating psychologically safe and open environments.

2. **Kim Scott** – *Radical Candor*: Provides guidance on balancing candor with care in feedback, helping leaders give honest feedback while respecting employees' feelings and motivations.

3. **Daniel Coyle** – *The Culture Code*: Explores how leaders can foster a culture of belonging, psychological safety, and team cohesion through intentional practices.

4. **Simon Sinek** – *Leaders Eat Last* and *Start with Why*: Sinek's books emphasize trust-building, purpose-driven leadership, and creating environments where people feel secure and motivated.

5. **Amy Edmondson** – *The Fearless Organization*: Research on psychological safety and its importance for innovation, teamwork, and employee engagement has shaped many organizational strategies.

6. **Daniel Goleman** – *Emotional Intelligence* and *Working with Emotional Intelligence*: Goleman's work provides a framework for understanding how emotional intelligence impacts leadership, communication, and teamwork.

ABOUT THE AUTHOR

A former Human Resource Director and Counselor for Adolescents, Laura Smith has over 25 years of experience working with a diverse, complex workforce. Her focus has always been the importance of effective communication and promotion of a positive workplace environment. Smith's knowledge also extends to working with complex issues in the workplace such as mental health concerns, substance abuse, training sensitive and fragile employees, and other difficult encounters that employers face on a daily basis. Her goal is to create a series "The Employer's Voice" condensed books that focus on key topics employers face and how to overcome those challenging situations.